Creating Connections

Creating Connections

How to Lead a Family Child Care Support Group

To Carolyn ~
What a pleasure to share
this with you ~ a
shared leader at heart!
All the Best!
Joan Laurion

Joan Laurion

Cherie Schmiedicke

Cherie
Schmiedicke
I can see the
strength & wisdom
in your soft-
spoken manner.
the best to you as
you consider your
work options!
Cherie

Redleaf Press
St. Paul, Minnesota
www.redleafpress.org

Published by Redleaf Press
a division of Resources for Child Caring
10 Yorkton Court
St. Paul, MN 55117
Visit us online at www.redleafpress.org.

Cover designed by Cathy Spengler
Interior typeset in Adobe Palatino and Adobe Myriad Pro
and designed by Dorie McClelland

Redleaf Press books are available at a special discount when purchased in bulk for special premiums and sales promotions. For details, contact the sales manager at 800-423-8309.

Library of Congress Cataloging-in-Publication Data

Laurion, Joan.
 Creating connections : how to lead a family child care support group / Joan Laurion, Cherie Schmiedicke.
    p. cm.
 Includes bibliographical references and index.
 ISBN-10: 1-929610-63-7 (pbk.)
 ISBN-13: 978-1-929610-63-1
 1. Family day care—Wisconsin—Madison. 2. Self-help groups—Wisconsin—Madison—Planning. I. Schmiedicke, Cherie. II. Title.
 HQ778.67.M33L38 2005
 362.71′2—DC22

                                    2004030203

Manufactured in the United States of America
12 11 10 09 08 07 06 05   1 2 3 4 5 6 7 8

We dedicate this book to the past and present members of Sojourn.

This group has been an important part of our lives—challenging us to do better care for children and their families, supporting us when we had struggles in our lives, and encouraging us when we had goals that seemed almost impossible to attain.

This level of support and camaraderie is our hope for every family child care support group.

It is with humble and sincere thanks that we dedicate this book to you. You are everywhere in this book and forever in our hearts.

Contents

Acknowledgments

THE MENTORS:

Dr. Boyd Rossing, for giving us a name for what we were doing and the encouragement to keep doing it

Sam Kaner, for that long, pivotal phone conversation and his generous support over the years

Cathy Toldi and Libby Backhuber, for their inspiring presentation of the concepts found in *Facilitator's Guide to Participatory Decision Making*

Kathy Modigliani, for understanding the connections, sharing the joy, and encouraging us every step of the way

THE SUPPORTERS:

Sherryl Hake and all the past and present Satellite Family Child Care staff, for their support of Sojourn, respite care, and accredited family child care in Madison, Wisconsin

Dorothy Conniff, Lorna Aaronson, Monica Host, and all the folks at the City of Madison Office of Community Services, for their commitment to high-quality family child care and for a training grant just when we needed it

Laura Satterfield, formerly with the Wisconsin Office of Child Care, for another important grant at the perfect moment

Chris Cross and Joan Matsalia, for the chance to present this material in three full-day workshops at National Association for Family Child Care (NAFCC) annual conferences

Carol Maurer, for her openness and support of family child care leadership trainings in Milwaukee, Wisconsin

Harriet Brown, for reading, editing, and powerful conversations

Beth Wallace and the late Kathy Kolb from Redleaf Press, for their guidance, patience, excitement, and belief in our project

THE FAMILY CHILD CARE PROVIDERS:

All family child care providers who have attended our workshops, for stories shared and lessons learned

Spectrum members, for an evening of memories and insights

METRO members, for those fun leadership training sessions in Milwaukee that included lots of laughs and great food

Denise Mirkin, for being the only original Sojourn member still in the group and still in the business of family child care—what a ride!

Kasia Bock-Leja and Sara Turner, for those long meetings at the coffee shop that turned into the first trainings and first handouts

THE FAMILY:

All of the children and families we had the honor to know in our family child care homes, for giving us the chance to learn and grow together

Manal and Cassie, and Dave, Peter, Laura, and Anna, for their loving moral support and for their invaluable expertise with computers!

Thank you to all.

One

Getting Connected

We need each other to test out ideas, to share

what we're learning, to help us see in new ways,

to listen to our stories.

Margaret Wheatley in *Leadership and the New Science*

In the quote on the preceding page, Margaret Wheatley sums up what this book is about: telling our story and sharing what we have learned about creating community, raising the quality of care for children, communicating and learning with other adults, and building leadership at all levels during our monthly family child care support group meetings. We hope that it will support your group as you test out these new ideas and that it will contribute to us all seeing family child care support groups and leadership development for family child care providers in new ways.

How We Started

We didn't know it at the time, but this book got started about fifteen years ago when we met as a group of family child care providers in a living room in Madison, Wisconsin. We had a vision of ourselves as mentors to each other for improving our work with children and families and as pioneers in the field of family child care.

At the time, the pioneering we were thinking about was figuring out how to hire a substitute caregiver together. We wanted to be able to take the personal and professional steps we dreamed about without quitting family child care. We needed someone to take our places from time to time. With the help of our parent organization, Satellite Family Child Care, we hired a substitute caregiver, Sherryl Hake. We formally contracted for half of her time and divided it up between us. We did the scheduling and billing ourselves and enjoyed many years of Sherryl's fantastic care for the children in our groups while we took better care of ourselves, attended college classes, and caught up on paperwork—barely, of course! That experience felt great so we kept meeting and challenging ourselves to learn how to support and mentor each other.

As in all stories, there are some embarrassing parts in our past. In those days, we called our group The Senior Providers because we were the long-term accredited providers within the Satellite Family Child Care system. We never felt comfortable with that name because it was a name that excluded so many of our colleagues. On top of this, Satellite required that the system screen and invite any new members into the Senior Providers group. This, of course, added to the elitism that everyone was uncomfortable with. Slowly, all that changed. Eventually, we decided upon a new name and requested that any provider be allowed to join. We ended up learning a lot about sharing leadership, building community, and supporting each other. That's what this book is about.

Our support group comprises about fifteen women. Several ethnicities and religions are represented among us. We live in a medium-sized midwestern city in the United States (Madison, Wisconsin). Some of us are single or single moms and many are married with kids. We have varied in age from twenty-five to sixty-five. We are from lower-middle to upper-middle income levels. Some are living on the income from family child care alone; most are two-income families. Our educational backgrounds are varied—from high school diplomas to associate degrees to advanced university degrees. Currently, all our members are heterosexual, although some of us have close lesbian and gay family members, friends, and clients. All of the providers in the group hold City of Madison family child care accreditation, which is comparable to National Association for Family Child Care (NAFCC) accreditation. We belong to a support system for family child care providers who are accredited or on the way to accreditation called Satellite Family Child Care. Now our support group is called "Sojourn," which means "staying in a different place for a while." Now providers and ex-providers, accredited and nonaccredited, are members of Sojourn.

WHAT'S THE DIFFERENCE?

Family Child Care Support Group

A family child care support group brings together a small group of family child care providers from the same local area for socializing, networking, peer mentoring, and grassroots leadership development, usually on a monthly basis. Support groups are usually run by providers.

Family Child Care Association

A family child care association is a formal membership organization brought together to meet political and organizational goals. Associations can have local, regional, state, national, and international components. The work of a family child care association revolves around impacting legislation and policy issues that affect family child care providers, children, and families. They often support quality improvement efforts and organize professional conferences. Associations are usually run by family child care leaders. Examples are the Wisconsin Family Child Care Association (WFCCA) and the National Association for Family Child Care (NAFCC).

Family Child Care System

Family child care systems are formal membership organizations. Systems have their own rules defining quality standards for the children's care or providers' training and/or about other specific conditions for membership. More and more, the quality standard of a family child care system is NAFCC accreditation or fulfillment of a comparable set of requirements. Systems usually offer their members services such as substitute care, training, referrals, and mediation. Systems can be very large, like the U.S. Marine Corps Family Child Care System around the world, or very small, like our Satellite Family Child Care system in Madison, Wisconsin, which has 75 members. Systems are usually run by a professional staff.

Family Child Care Network

A family child care network loosely describes a variety of relatively small, local family child care organizations. They bring together a group of providers for a specific purpose usually having to do with support, quality improvement, and/or education. Networks may provide some of the services of a system like offering equipment rotation and organizing support groups but without the standards and supervisory component that systems have. Networks are usually run by a professional staff.

Checking In

We started out meeting monthly, with snacks and a program like most family child care support groups. What probably moved us along in a different direction were two things. First, we decided to require attendance. We knew from our work with children that if we were to become trusted colleagues, we needed to actually be together on a regular basis. We knew we had to earn each other's trust and that without it, we would not come to depend on each other.

Second, as an afterthought, we decided to "check in" at the beginning of every meeting. One of our members had been in a feminist choir in the 1970s and she remembered that going around the circle of women at every meeting had been really cool. What she forgot was that check-in should be timed! We had many somewhat painful ninety-minute check-in sessions before we chose to manage our time together and limit everyone to the same number of minutes. Now check-in takes about thirty minutes.

The gift that those early check-ins gave us was the experience of getting to know each other very well. We treasured the experience of speaking and hearing about the details of our lives and work in such a focused and respectful way. We could tell that we were on to something, but we did not know what it was yet. We didn't know that years later, we would talk about the importance of community-building activities like check-in as if they had always been a part of our vocabulary and understanding. We stumbled along trying programs and no programs; timing and no timing; leading and no leading; business and more business. And we kept checking in.

Shared Leadership

Finally, in a class at the University of Wisconsin, Joan learned that what we were stumbling through had a name and that people wrote books about it! It was called "nonhierarchical" or "shared" leadership. Four of our members formed a little ad hoc committee and devoured the *Facilitator's Guide to Participatory Decision Making* (1996) by Kaner, Lind, Toldi, Fisk, and Berger, and cobbled together a seven-session training program for Satellite support group leaders that taught them more than it taught their good-spirited participants. Sam Kaner, who is a senior associate with Community at Work, a think tank and consulting firm that specializes in participatory group decision making, helped us to bring Community at Work trainers Cathy Toldi and Libby Backhuber to Madison to train twenty-five of us from Madison-area support groups in group facilitation and inclusive decision making.

The next facilitators of our support group worked very hard to model good facilitation. They talked on the phone and met between meetings to plan the agenda and the activities they wanted to try out. Over coffee, they talked, argued, and laughed together as they struggled with the new concepts and skills. The facilitation that Kasia Bock-Leja and Sara Turner taught themselves and implemented with us over the next four years quietly modeled to everyone how to facilitate calmly, gracefully, and with transparency. A turning point came when one of them said to the group, "I've realized that I don't have to be nervous about facilitating the meeting. I have all of you helping me. We'll figure it out together as we go along." We finally trusted each other and the process of shared leadership.

Purpose and Process

Every once in a while, people would ask us, "What exactly does your group do?" We had to answer that we are not much of a "doing" group. Instead, we were a group that supported "doing" individuals. We worked hard at raising the quality of child care in our family child care homes through timely support for caregivers and at building leadership skills in each one of our members at every meeting.

Through the years, we have intentionally experimented with everything: open discussion and alternatives to open discussion; eating last, eating first, and eating in the middle; keeping roles and changing roles; socializing before the meeting and socializing after the meeting; etc.

We started offering training at the local, state, and national levels on shared leadership in family child care support groups. Our participants at those conferences—bless their hearts—were enthusiastic and supportive. They especially appreciated the activity we call "Two Lists," which follows. A lightbulb goes on for just about everyone who sees what is on the two lists of what providers value most in a family child care support group. Strategies for leading family child care support groups become much clearer when you know what your priorities are.

activity
_____

TWO LISTS

Purpose of this activity: To help groups define what is most important to them in family child care support groups.

When to use it: When introducing the ideas of community and trust building.

Materials needed: Flip chart on an easel, markers.

What to do: Set up the easel and flip chart in front of the group, with the flip chart facing away from the group so they can't see what you're writing. Ask the group to help make a long list of all the things that family child care support groups do (or should do, or would like to do). As members name the activities and roles, write down each idea on the flip chart, putting the items that have to do with relationships and support in one list and logistics, projects, training, money, field trips, etc., in the other list. The lists will probably look something like the following diagram.

Sharing stories about the children	*Advocacy*
Laughing together	*Week of the Young Child activities*
Getting suggestions about handling different issues	*Fund-raising*
Eating together	*Trainings*
Socializing with adults	*Toy-lending library*
Being with others who "get" what I do	*Field trips*

After the group has mentioned all of its ideas, ask the providers in the group to name the thing that is most important to them at their support group. It helps to say, "What is the bottom line? What do you need most from your support group?" Star the responses they give with a different colored marker. You may have to make additions to the lists. Remember to star them.

After the providers have shared all their ideas and you have starred all the items, turn the flip chart around so everyone can see the two lists and the stars.

First ask, "What do the two lists represent? How are the items grouped?" Then say, "The stars show the things that you said were most important to you. Where are the stars?"

If your group is like every other group we've worked with, almost all the stars will be on the relationship and support side of the page (i.e., the left side of the chart above). Remind the participants that all the items are important functions of family child care support groups but that it is clear from the two lists that the personally supportive aspects of the group are what providers value most highly. We can have all these other things happening in our family child care support groups, but we need to be absolutely sure to figure out ways to provide opportunities for building strong relationships and support.

Follow this activity with a community-building activity—eating, playing a game, or checking in.

How to Use This Book

So, welcome to our book about creating connections with each other and leading family child care groups. Here are the things that we hope you will understand better after reading this book:

- Community building

- Shared leadership

- Roles in shared leadership

- Inclusive decision making

- Facilitative skills

- Creating an agenda and timekeeping

- Alternatives to open discussion

- Supporting providers taking action

Like any workshop, we have a few housekeeping items to cover before we get started.

We arranged the book in an order that we thought would be useful and logical, but we also know that you may need several of the skills at the same time. You may find yourself bouncing around a fair amount. If your group is already established, you will want to pick the area that you'd like to address first and start there. It may be chapter 10, Making Discussions Worthwhile, that you use first. There is a road map in chapter 2, Sharing Leadership, that gives you another way of looking at the organization of the book and how you could best work your way through.

We want you to look for the personal stories from providers that are contained within each chapter. These are stories we have gathered from our support group and other support groups we have worked with. We hope these stories will help illustrate the concepts with the words and examples from "real life" providers just like you!

Almost all of our readers will be women, so, throughout the book, we refer to family child care providers as women and use the pronouns "she" and "her." We welcome warmly the few men who may be in our ranks and ask for your understanding when we use feminine pronouns. We want you to know that you are included too.

Likewise, we sometimes refer to parents or families without adding guardians, grandparents, or caregivers to the list. We realize that children are cared for by many other people besides their parents and that family child care providers need to partner with anyone in that role. Please mentally add all those wonderful people who care for children when we use the shorter term at times.

The bathrooms are down the hall and feel free to grab a bite to eat whenever you'd like . . . here we go!

More Reading

Center For Child Care Workforce. 1999. *Creating better family child care jobs: Model work standards.* Washington, D.C.: Center for Child Care Workforce.

Excellent overview of quality standards for a family child care work place. The need for support, mentoring, and leadership development for providers is highlighted. The appendices dealing with "fair cost of care" and other family child care business considerations would be great for discussion starters.

Kontos, Susan, C. Howes, M. Shinn, and E. Galinsky. 1994. *Quality in family child care and relative care.* New York: Teachers College Press.

This important study documented a positive correlation between providers who offer a higher quality of care for children and providers who participate in family child care support groups or networks.

Two

Sharing Leadership

Sharing leadership means every person pays attention to what needs doing or saying next and participates in doing his/her share. . . . Responsibility also shifts from moment to moment and task by task. Shared responsibility is based on the trust that someone will come forward to provide whatever the (group) needs next: helping each other take action, calling for silence, or offering the next meeting place.

Christina Baldwin in *Calling the Circle*

Over the years, as we've focused on the important work of raising the quality and professionalism of family child care, technical assistance staff and family child care providers alike have tended to organize meetings of family child care providers around formal training. Usually, this has meant that meetings are planned in advance and an "expert" is invited to teach the group.

It has come to be considered good professional practice for a family child care support group leader to plan a year's worth of meetings; arrange for speakers, location, dates, times, and snacks; and then send out a schedule for the year to all the members of the group. This model has been even further legitimized by some specific state licensing requirements concerning continuing education hours. Some states award training hours to providers only when outside trainers are present at the family child care support group meetings.

In rural areas where training opportunities are offered less frequently and it may take hours to get to training events, formal training with a speaker addressing a prearranged topic may be a very important part of the family child care support group meeting. If your group is one of those, we invite you to read chapter 5 to get some ideas on how to practice shared leadership and offer important formal training to your members at the same time.

Currently, there is less reason to continue this traditional training model in our family child care support groups. In most areas of the country, excellent educational programs for family child care providers are available online; at conferences; at colleges and universities; at technical colleges; through local Resource & Referral agencies (R&Rs); through the Child Development Associate (CDA), the National Association for Family Child Care (NAFCC), and other accreditation training; and through community organizations. Participation in these educational programs, especially credit-bearing classes, is extremely important for raising the quality of care in family child care homes. What isn't available elsewhere, however, is the opportunity to create friendships and trust with other providers over time; to talk over current issues and challenges with trusted colleagues; to participate in informal peer mentoring; and to build grassroots leadership capacity among family child care professionals. The traditional organizational structure that we have been describing is planned and directed by one person or a small group of people. It is called hierarchical or directive leadership. In this model, one person is in charge of the meeting, and often someone presents expert knowledge on a given topic. A diagram of directive leadership in a family child care support group (or any organization) would look like diagram A.

In this model, transferring information from the leader and/or trainer to the members or learners is most important. Building relationships, sharing ideas among the members of the group, and making space for discussion between the members and with the trainer is a lower priority.

Excellent trainers will build discussion activities into their presentations and will encourage feedback and challenging questions from all members of the group, making the model less directive and more facilitative. Members will be more engaged with the trainer and with each other as they consider the topic at hand. A diagram of that model would look like diagram B.

A Model for Family Child Care Support Groups: Shared Leadership

In shared or facilitative leadership, all members of the group share responsibility for raising discussion topics, and all members are invited to discuss, learn, and reflect on a given topic with other members of the group. This model can also be called nonhierarchical leadership. A nonhierarchical model where leadership, power, knowledge, values, opinions, and experiences are shared can be represented this way:

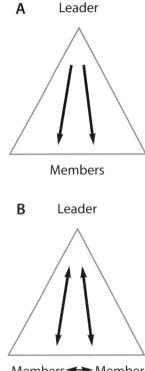

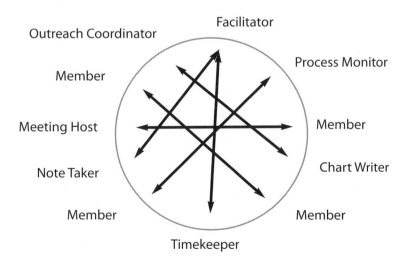

In this book, we explain how to lead your family child care support group using shared leadership principles. The goal of this model differs from the goals of directive leadership and most formalized training, requiring strategies that may not be as familiar to you.

We propose these long-range goals for family child care support groups:

- Establish positive, supportive relationships among members of the group.

- Raise the quality of care for children in the support group members' family child care programs and help create positive and reciprocal provider-parent relationships.

- Increase leadership capacity in all members of the family child care support group.

We propose four strategies for reaching these long-term goals:

- Include intentional community-building activities and individual check-in at every support group meeting.

- Make the providers' own current burning issues the main topics for discussion, learning, and reflection at every meeting. These issues could include ones having to do with children, families, environment, curriculum, business, and professional development.

- Intentionally use facilitative skills in open discussion, and try out alternatives to open discussion to address providers' burning issues.

- Adopt shared leadership as the leadership model for family child care support groups.

Why is shared leadership a good fit for family child care support groups?

Our experience has shown that there are a number of sound reasons to use shared leadership within family child care support groups. Here are some of them:

- Family child care support groups usually meet only once a month.

- Many family child care providers already practice shared leadership.

- Most family child care providers are women.

- Providers come with varying degrees of self-confidence.

- Building trust requires involvement from everyone.

Family child care support groups usually meet only once a month.

Family child care providers must make the most of their time together. For providers, this time is precious time for connecting with other professionals, sharing joys, and addressing current challenges. Family child care providers do not have the daily informal interaction with other colleagues that most professionals enjoy. They do not have a chance to learn and reflect with one another in an informal way from day to day. Every support group meeting should intentionally include time and structure for reconnecting and sharing even if formal training is part of the meeting.

Many family child care providers already practice shared leadership.

Family child care providers who provide high-quality early care and education practice shared leadership with the children they care for. A family child care provider who offers high-quality care for children carefully builds strong relationships among the children of her group and makes sure that all the children get their fair share of time and attention from her and the other children. She teaches children to take responsibility for themselves and also to watch out for one another. She asks that everyone be respected and included. No one is in charge all the time, and everyone is responsible for the well-being of the group. Here are some examples of shared leadership in a family child care home:

- Often a child becomes the leader for a while. When a child asks to read a particular book, he is leading the group for that moment. Later, two other children may have a dispute and then they become the leaders.

- When the provider needs to make a phone call, all the children are asked to be quiet for a moment and the provider's needs come first.

- When it's time to hurry across a street, a skilled family child care provider understands that directive leadership is sometimes necessary and does not hesitate to take charge at those times.

The process of valuing and feeling comfortable with sharing power and passing leadership back and forth is already a natural part of a family child care provider's understanding and skill. Practicing this in her support group will not be a new concept, but it will present new challenges and opportunities for personal and professional growth.

Most family child care providers are women.

Research in this area gives us perspective on the ways women tend to learn best. We know that women tend to construct knowledge for themselves by testing new material against their own knowledge and experiences and the experiences of others they trust. When women consider new material, they often think about how it relates to their own lives and the specific people and events around them.

When choosing an educational process for groups made up of mostly women, we should take into consideration this preference for what Belenky, Clinchy, Goldberger, and Tarule call "connected learning" in their book *Women's Ways of Knowing* (1986). The group's process needs to include interacting among members and sharing experiences related to the new material.

We are not suggesting that a connected learning model is valuable only for women. Research addressing women's learning does not tell us about differences between the ways women and men learn. The research on women's learning only tells us how women tend to construct their knowledge. The implications for practice that come from this body of research are very similar to best practices for adult education in general. For men in family child care support groups, these strategies will be appropriate, meaningful, and effective too.

Providers come with varying degrees of self-confidence.

Some women, and particularly women in low-prestige, low-paying jobs like family child care, may have learned to quiet their own feelings and voices. Some family child care providers hesitate to state their own needs, opinions, and desires. They may fear that conflict will hurt the relationships that are so important to them. Others may have learned to be overly defensive to protect themselves.

Shared leadership within the family child care support group encourages women to build a trusting community where they can practice speaking what is true for them without being apologetic and without fear. Members gain confidence, self-esteem, and leadership skills within the safety of the group. We believe that this ability can transfer in a powerful way to other parts of caregivers' lives. It can raise the quality of care for children in their groups, improve relationships and informal educational experiences with parents, and encourage caregivers to take other important leadership roles in their communities and in the field of early-childhood care and education.

Building trust requires involvement from everyone.

When each member of the group knows she is equally responsible for helping the meeting be successful, negative behaviors like monopolizing, gossiping, and stereotyping can be addressed more effectively. When members think that only the leader is responsible for how the meeting goes, they will defer to her and hesitate to take action to improve the meetings. They will not feel they have the authority or power to encourage positive relationships among the members. When the group implements shared leadership and learns facilitation strategies that include everyone, all members realize that they have not only the responsibility but also the skills for making meetings positive and useful for all.

What I appreciate the most about being a facilitator in a group that uses the shared leadership model is that the facilitator is really part of a leadership team. That team takes full responsibility for the smooth operation of the group, but because there is not just one leader, the entire group begins to take responsibility for itself.

Using Multiple Leadership Skills

Whenever you teach new skills or new concepts to children or adults, a more directive style is needed at first. Those of you reading this book will need to use directive leadership to influence your family child care support group to try some of the new ideas presented here. You'll need to take the lead and use a combination of building strong relationships with your family child care colleagues, communicating your vision, suggesting a plan, and expressing your enthusiasm! As you lead your group through the first steps of learning about community building, facilitative skills, and shared leadership, you'll need to make lots of decisions about how, when, and what to propose to the group.

WHEN ORGANIZING THE GROUP, SOME QUESTIONS TO CONSIDER ARE:

In what order shall we introduce these concepts, roles, and strategies with our group?

How shall we introduce them and practice them with the group?

How fast shall we introduce them?

Every group will be different. But in most groups, learning facilitation skills, strategies for shared leadership, and best practices in educating adults (especially adult women) will all overlap. You'll be learning several things at once as you did when you started your family child care business. You couldn't start your business without jumping into child development, curriculum planning, home improvement, and running a small business all at once. They are interrelated, and each demands at least some attention from the get-go. It's the same with shared leadership. In order to check in, which is a basic activity in most shared leadership groups, you'll need to learn something about timekeeping, community building, and facilitation.

Though these topics overlap, you'll need to prioritize what is most important. Your group will learn many interrelated shared leadership concepts over the years, but you can't do them all thoroughly at once. You will need to start learning some of these roles and strategies and leave others until you are further down the road. Wherever you decide to begin, it will be important to start slowly with two or three ideas. Get feedback from the group about how those are working. Expect to make changes several times before things feel exactly right for your group.

Remember, too, that learning together and struggling through some difficulties will help your group feel closer and stronger in the long run. Our group experimented for years. We knew that we wanted a family child care support group that acknowledged our expertise and our ability to provide one another with support and mentoring, but we did not have a clear idea how to get there. We figured that it required trusting one another and being able to learn from one another, so we started simply—with check-in, a facilitator, a timekeeper, and community-building activities. The following list will help your group get started. We encourage you to give it a go. It's worth it!

SUGGESTED ORDER FOR LEARNING SHARED LEADERSHIP

To get started:	Chapter
• Why and how of community building	3
• Eating and socializing together	3
• Focused check-in	4
• Collecting burning issues	4
• Creating an agenda at the meeting	4
• Sharing time with a speaker	5
• Facilitator and facilitation skills	6, 7, 8
• Meeting host	8
• Timekeeper and timekeeper skills	8

Making decisions together:	
• Making decisions about logistics	6
• Choosing group standards for interaction	6
• Participatory decision making	6

Nuts and bolts:	
• Why and how of shared leadership	2
• Opening/closing ritual	3
• Group members' role	8
• Outreach coordinator and coordinator and telephone tree	9
• Note taker and minutes	9
• Chart writer and chart-writing skills	9
• Facilitating open discussion	10
• Facilitating some alternatives to open discussion	11

Going deeper:	
• Meeting needs of adult women learners	2, 12
• Unfocused check-in	3
• Refrain from giving advice during open discussion	10
• Process monitor	9
• Facilitating more alternatives to open discussion	11

More Reading

Belenky, Mary Field, Blythe McVicker Clinchy, Nancy Rule Goldberger, and Jill Mattuck Tarule. 1986. *Women's ways of knowing: The development of self, voice, and mind.* New York: HarperCollins.

Gilligan, Carol. 1982. *In a different voice: Psychological theory and women's development.* Cambridge: Harvard University Press.

Both these books laid the groundwork for understanding the way women tend to learn best and how their participation in their own learning changes over time. Belenky's explanation of how "voice" relates to learning was an "aha" moment for us.

Three

Building Community and Trust

Communities have sometimes been referred to as leaderless

groups. It is more accurate, however, to say that a community

is a group of all leaders.

M. Scott Peck in *The Different Drum*

Even though family child care support groups serve many valuable functions, providers always say that the most cherished feature of the group is friendship and trust. Family child care providers need trusted colleagues in their family child care support group for sharing experiences and support. They look to one another for honesty, understanding, and acceptance. They thrive in the respect and appreciation they offer one another.

What Is Community Building?

Creating the space and opportunity to become honest and trusted friends and colleagues is called community building. It is the most important part of forming and maintaining a family child care support group.

Building community and trust is an ongoing process. In community, members expect to enjoy themselves and one another and to share commitment to the well-being of the group. Trust grows when members feel respected, included, and appreciated. Trust allows people to listen carefully, participate honestly, and reflect together openly.

Remember that family child care providers usually work alone and are not forming day-to-day friendships with colleagues as other professionals do. Many receive important support from family, friends, and the children's parents, but the friendship and mentoring that is shared among family child care providers is satisfying and unique. In order for providers to form trusting and supportive relationships that will allow them to share and learn with one another on a regular basis, we need to dedicate time at every meeting to community- and trust-building activities.

I have so many good memories being on field trips to the fire station or the pumpkin patch with other providers and their groups. Since parents would often be along on these trips, I felt such a level of professionalism when the parents would see all of the providers doing quality care. And now we have so many shared memories together as support group members too—these memories really strengthen our ability to support one another during our support group meetings.

Learning how to build community in a family child care support group gives providers leadership skills that are valuable outside of the group. Learning about intentional community and trust building in the family child care support group can give providers ideas about ways to invite parents into a more trusting relationship around the positive development of their children. Building community and trust is also a critical element in successful community organizations and advocacy groups. Providers who understand community building know that having fun, getting to know one another as individuals, acknowledging and honoring differences, and beginning to trust one another make working together and decision making much easier no matter what the organization or relationship.

So how do we build community and trust among adults? As we mentioned in chapter 2, providers who offer high-quality family child care know a lot about this already because they are doing it all the time with children. They know to strive for a strong sense of family and community among the children in order for them to establish strong relationships and enjoy learning together. Providers who offer high-quality care help children have fun together; they encourage children to listen and talk with one another; they make sure children have shared experiences; and they take care that the children learn to acknowledge and respect one another's differences.

All those activities are similar to the ways adults build community. For this reason, many of the following community-building activities for family child care support groups will look very familiar. The activities are in order, from those that are most common and safe to activities that you will want to do after your group members have become more comfortable and trusting with one another. We have grouped the community-building activities like this:

1. Eating together

2. Socializing

3. Having fun, playing games, and laughing together

   - Getting-to-know-you games

     - Purse Peeking

     - Name-by-Name—a listening game for a group

     - Group Up—an active getting-to-know-you game

     - Three Truths and One Lie—getting-past-first-perceptions game

     - Hobby Hunt—a talk-to-everyone game

     - Anyone Who!—a very active getting-to-know-you game

4. Creating shared rituals—opening, closing, welcoming, and good-bye rituals

   • Welcoming New Members

5. Honoring and appreciating one another's differences

   • Sharing symbolic objects

   • Learning about one another's personality and communication styles

     • Four Corners—a personality-style game

6. Expressing appreciation to one another

7. Going to conferences or on retreat together

8. Making decisions and learning about shared leadership together

9. Playing leadership games

   • Back-to-Back—a communication game with drawing

   • Claytionary—a hands-on observation game

   • Tiny Teach—a leadership game

   • "I've Got the Power"—a very active shared leadership game

10. Playing challenging shared leadership games

   • Stand Up—an active collaborative game for pairs

   • Pass the Hoop—an active game for a group

COMMUNITY-BUILDING ACTIVITIES

Eating together

Eating together gives group members a chance for relaxed, informal talking and sharing. Time should be set aside at every meeting for eating a snack or light dinner together and socializing. Consider having a potluck or preparing a meal together. Many groups like to celebrate the diverse cultural and ethnic backgrounds of their members by sharing foods and recipes from their families.

Socializing

The family child care support group meeting is one of the few places where providers can share the precious and hilarious tales of family child care and know that their listeners appreciate the depth of the story right along with them. Informal socializing, with the understanding that there will be no gossiping later, allows personal sharing, listening, and connecting among providers. It is critical for community building. When providers don't get time for socializing, they tend to have more side conversations and more trouble staying focused on the group discussion. We suggest planning for a half hour of social time before the official meeting starts, and plan for fifteen to twenty minutes of eating and socializing during the meeting.

Having fun, playing games, and laughing together

Be sure to take time to laugh and have fun together. Playing interactive getting-to-know-you games, learning dance steps together, singing, or looking at one another's baby pictures are just a few of the possibilities. To get you started, we've collected some of our favorite games. Many of these games are adapted from *Quicksilver* (1995) by Karl Rohnke and Steve Butler.

Purse Peeking

Ask each person to look in her bag and pick out one thing that means something important to her. Turn to a partner and take turns telling one another about the thing you chose and why it is important. Each person gets sixty to ninety seconds to tell her story.

Name-by-Name—adapted from Harrison Snow's book, *Indoor-Outdoor Team-Building Games for Trainers*, 1997

Stand in a circle. Each person in turn says her first name out loud. If the group members know one another, you could suggest that everyone say her middle name instead. If someone can't hear, she should yell, "Repeat!" After all the names are said, announce the challenge, which is for people to rearrange themselves so that they're in alphabetical order by name. Show where the alphabet starts and ends. Tell the group that there is no talking, signing, or gesturing allowed. Helpful pointing or repositioning is fine.

When the circle has reformed, have everyone say their names again. If people are out of sequence, they can move a second time. Then have the group say their names again and repeat until the sequence is correct. At the end, ask the group what helped them. What does this say about getting people to listen carefully, in general?

Group Up—adapted from Harrison Snow's book, *Indoor-Outdoor Team-Building Games for Trainers,* 1997

The group stands and mingles around the room. The leader names a characteristic, like "number of people in your family." Everyone quickly gets into groups with others who have the same answer to that characteristic. When the group is settled, the leader can ask each group to name its shared characteristic. Then the leader states another characteristic. Other suggestions:

• Number of children enrolled in your group

• Time you get up in the morning

• Number of car seats in your car

- Ages of your children

- Favorite time of day

- Pets in your house

- Pet peeve about family child care

Three Truths and One Lie

Give each person a piece of paper and a pencil. Tell members to write three things that are true about themselves and one that is a lie—in random order. Make the truths things that others would probably not know. Ask members to pair up with someone they do not know well and exchange papers. Each person takes a turn guessing which things are true about the other person and which are false.

Hobby Hunt

Before the meeting, write a list of hobbies on a sheet of paper with a line after each where someone can write her name. Make enough copies of the list so that everyone in the group has her own. Ask the group to canvass one another about their hobbies and print members' names after the hobbies they enjoy.

You can vary this game by choosing different topics. For example:

- Make a list of obscure facts, like: "I shampoo my hair every day," or "I have a toothbrush in my car," or "I've driven a semi-truck."

- Make a list of family descriptions, like: "I have four children," or "I am a twin," or "I've been married twice."

- Make a list of work-related topics, like: "I've been a waitress," or "I had my first job before I was 10," or "I've earned money working with animals."

- Make a list by mixing up all of the above.

After ten or fifteen minutes, ask if anyone still has a blank she can't fill. You can also share a few items with the entire group by asking, "So who has a toothbrush in her car?"

Anyone Who!

As you stand in the center, ask everyone to pull her chair into a large circle around you. Counting yourself, this means that there is one less chair than people in the group. Explain that you will say something that is true about you and that everyone for whom this is also true needs to get up and find another chair. No one can go to a chair that is right next to her on either side. For example, if you have been hunting, you could say, "Anyone who has ever gone hunting." Then everyone who has been hunting should get up and find a different chair. This is your clue to find an empty chair too. The person who is left without a chair becomes the one to go to the center and say, "Anyone who . . ." The game speeds up and gets more competitive and fun from here on!

Creating shared rituals

Creating rituals for opening and closing the meeting, welcoming new members, and saying good-bye creates strong connections and allows members to practice leadership.

Keep all these rituals short and simple, but do keep them. As an opening ritual, someone could read a favorite quote. For closing the meeting, a quick go-around lets everyone share her last thoughts and appreciations with her colleagues. Be sure to acknowledge with words or a gesture when a provider visits, joins, or leaves the group. A card, simple symbolic gift, poem, or song is perfect.

Welcoming New Members

Here's one idea for a symbolic way to welcome a new member into your group. Have each member write a personal message to the new member on a strip of paper. The strips are stapled together into a chain along with a strip from the new member, symbolically linking the new member to the existing group.

Honoring and appreciating one another's differences

It is important to address ways that group members differ in race, class, education, ethnicity, age, religion, sexual orientation, urban/rural residence, etc., in a straightforward way. The goal is to unlearn stereotypes and work with people from different backgrounds in a mutually beneficial way. Informal conversation and intentional dialogue are best, of course. Here are two other ways that you might approach these discussions in your group.

Share Symbolic Objects

Each member brings an object that is important to her because it symbolizes the way that she is stereotyped by her friends or family or by the culture around her. Each person takes a turn describing the object and her experiences in any way she would like. The rest of the group listens. Each member places the object in the center of the circle as part of a temporary collage of the group members' experiences.

Explore Personality Styles

Taking a personality or perceptual-patterns survey together is interesting and fun. Two we have used are the Matrixx System® Colors survey and Dawna Markova's perceptual-patterns survey in *How Your Child Is Smart* (1992).

Four Corners—adapted from Harrison Snow's book, *Indoor-Outdoor Team-Building Games for Trainers*, 1997

Playing the game Four Corners is another way to explore the different communication and personality styles of members in your group.

Write these four words on separate pieces of flip chart paper and tape them up in four different areas of the room:

Organization	Understanding
Relationships	Action

Ask your group members to stand near the word that they most relate to. Give each group five to seven minutes to discuss among themselves why they chose the word they did and how that strength helps them in the work they do. Have each group explain to the whole group what they discussed. After all the groups have explained the importance of their word to the others, ask if anyone would like to change groups, and have her explain why.

Possible debriefing questions: What was surprising to you about what other groups had to say? Which group is the most challenging for you to work with and why? Which group do you work with best and why? What questions would you like to ask other groups to help you understand how they feel and think? What does this tell us about working with children? How does it inform our work with parents?

Expressing appreciation to one another

Naturally expressing appreciation for words, actions, caring, growth, courage, etc., can be done informally whenever the occasion arises. Your group can also encourage some formal appreciating. One way is to finish the meeting by thanking the meeting host and having each member say something appreciative about the person sitting to her left. Another option is to put all the members' names into a container and pick one at each meeting. Everyone present at that meeting offers one appreciative comment about the person whose name was chosen. Be sure to make expressing appreciation a normal part of your group's being together.

Going to conferences or on retreat together

Pick a special event or location that offers your group members the ideal setting for what they'd like to do together. You may choose to go to a conference together or to plan an extended training opportunity, a longer community-building activity, or time to focus on a group project. Be sure to allow time for personal relaxation and having fun together.

Making decisions and learning about shared leadership together

Making decisions in a way that includes everyone's point of view and strives for a high level of agreement from all members of the group can also serve to build trust and community among the members. Chapter 6 outlines several basic strategies for participatory decision making. You can find many more decision-making concepts and strategies in *Facilitator's Guide to Participatory Decision Making* (1996) by Kaner, Lind, Toldi, Fisk, and Berger.

Start with a low-stakes decision without a deadline. Our support group challenged itself to learn some of these processes as we chose a new name for our group. We had been called The Senior Providers, which made people think that you had to be over 65 to join! It was embarrassing, but no one was requiring us to find a new name and we had no deadline for picking one.

It took us two years of activities, on and off, to come to a decision! We drew pictures and did visioning. We brainstormed and formed an ad hoc committee. We multi-voted (see chapter 9) many times. In the end, we had our new name, we had a toolbox full of participatory decision-making experiences, and we had the trust that comes from all that honest sharing and debating.

Playing leadership games

Team-building games, as they are sometimes called, can stimulate interesting and valuable discussion about different aspects of leadership. To make this happen, debriefing is important. Suggestions for debriefing are at the end of each activity. Keep it short and simple. A good debriefing ending for any game is: Are there any last thoughts on this activity?

Back-to-Back—adapted from Harrison Snow's book, *Indoor-Outdoor Team-Building Games for Trainers,* 1997

Group members pair up and sit back-to-back. Without showing the second member of the pair, the leader gives the first member of the pair a sheet of paper with a simple figure drawn on it. The second member of the pair gets a sheet of paper and a pen or marker. The person with the figure is the coach. She guides her partner in drawing the figure without letting her see the original. The coach can use words that include symbols and metaphors but not geometric designs. For example, the words "square" and "circle" are not allowed. Instead, the coach could say "like a box" or "plate-shaped." The person drawing may ask questions for clarification. After about ten minutes, let the pairs compare their drawings.

Debriefing: This exercise emphasizes the challenges of communication. Ask the group to discuss what the coaches said that helped with the drawing. What did they say that made it more confusing? What did the drawers do that helped the coaches? What does this tell us about communication?

If you have time, reverse the roles, provide a new figure, and repeat the game. Debrief as before, asking how people changed the way they described or questioned because of the previous conversation.

Claytionary—adapted from *Quicksilver* (1995) by Karl Rohnke and Steve Butler

This game is like Pictionary™ except that it is played with playdough. Divide the group into smaller groups of three to six people. Give each group some playdough. Each group selects a modeler to start. All the modelers come over to the leader and read the first word or phrase. Each modeler returns to her group and sculpts the first word or phrase, without talking. Group members try to guess what the modeler is sculpting. As soon as one group guesses the correct answer, another modeler is chosen from each group and goes up to the leader for the next word or phrase. The game continues until each person has had at least one turn. Suggestions for words:

- Animals: python, kangaroo, dolphin, flamingo

- Famous places: Grand Sphinx, Arc de Triomphe, Mount Rushmore, Grand Canyon

• Things around the house: vacuum cleaner, bicycle, whisk, iron

Debriefing: Ask the group to show how the activity went with a thumbs-up or thumbs-down scale. Ask those with thumbs up to explain what happened in their groups that made the activity successful. Ask the thumbs-down folks what happened that made it unsuccessful.

Other questions: Was there anything frustrating about this activity for you? What part of this activity was particularly satisfying? What does this tell us about hands-on activities? About leadership?

Tiny Teach—adapted from Harrison Snow's book, *Indoor-Outdoor Team-Building Games for Trainers,* 1997

Ask the group members to pair up and teach one another something that will take only two to five minutes to learn. It could be a song, a phrase in another language, a dance step, etc. Remind the group to switch after five minutes for the second person's turn. Invite members to share what they learned with the whole group.

Debriefing questions: How did you feel at first about this activity? And now? How did you feel about the other person teaching you? How did you feel about sharing? What does this say about sharing knowledge and expertise within a group or an organization? With the parents you work with?

"I've Got the Power"—adapted from Harrison Snow's book, *Indoor-Outdoor Team-Building Games for Trainers,* 1997

This is a game like "Simon Says" except it uses warm-up-type exercises. Explain that the leader will say, "I've got the power" and start doing a stretching exercise. Everyone else should copy that movement until the leader or someone else says, "I've got the power," and starts another stretching exercise. Then everyone follows that person. Tell the group that the game keeps going until everyone

THE THUMBS SCALE

• Thumbs straight up means the activity was a total success with lots of teamwork or careful observation.

• Thumbs down means there was no teamwork or observation.

• Thumbs to the side means there was some teamwork, but there could be more.

has taken the power at least once. If no one takes over from you, yell, "I've got the power," and start doing push-ups or something difficult, and that will encourage someone else to take the power!

Debrief by using the thumbs scale (see previous page). Consider asking how it felt to yell out, "I've got the power" and take over the group. What did it feel like to have all eyes on you? What does this tell us about being a member of a group that shares leadership?

Playing challenging shared leadership games

Here are some very active leadership games that require physical activity, teamwork, and strategic thinking.

Stand Up—adapted from editor Andrew Fluegelman's book, *The New Games Book* (1976)

Two people sit on the ground back-to-back, knees bent and elbows linked, and then stand up together. They can do this a couple of times. Then ask the whole group to create groups of three people and do the same thing. Then groups of four and five. The more people who try to do this together, the more struggling, stumbling, and giggling there is.

Debriefing: Ask about the difference between standing up with one other person and standing up with four or more. Why was it more difficult? What does it take to stand up comfortably as a large group? How about going down? How does all this apply to working as a group in general?

Pass the Hoop—adapted from editor Andrew Fluegelman's book, *The New Games Book* (1976)

The group stands in a circle holding hands with two hula hoops hanging from two opposite pairs of clasped hands. Without letting go of hands, send the hula hoops around the circle—one clockwise and the other counterclockwise. Passing the hula hoops takes teamwork because only arms and bodies are used. For more fun, add more hula hoops.

Debrief with the thumbs scale (see page 33), asking how this activity worked in terms of reaching the goal. Did this activity work in terms of creativity? Why or why not? Using the thumbs scale, ask how people felt during this activity. Explain. What does this tell us about leadership? Teamwork?

Clearly, groups will need a particularly thoughtful dose of community and relationship building when they are newly forming or as they recover from a difficult period. But remember, community and relationship building are never over. You will want to tailor your community-building activities to what is best for your group at this time. No matter what stage you are at, community building needs to be an ongoing part of every family child care support meeting, just as it is an integral part of every day in a family child care home and every day with parents. If you attend to building strong, trusting relationships all the time, then when you need to make a decision, support a colleague, or advocate for legislation, your group will have the trust and inclusive relationships it needs to function at a very high level.

More Reading

Baldwin, Christina. 1994. *Calling the circle: The first and future culture.* New York: Bantam Books.

A look at how reflection and spirit-based groups apply community building and shared leadership.

Rohnke, Karl, and Steve Butler. 1995. *Quicksilver.* Dubuque, Iowa: Kendall/Hunt Publishing.

A book chock-a-block with games and icebreakers.

Snow, Harrison. 1997. *Indoor-outdoor team-building games for trainers.* New York: McGraw-Hill.

Excellent collection of activities that invite group reflection and learning about leadership and community development.

Four

Checking In and Creating the Agenda

When we acknowledge that our experiences with one another are important, when we stretch to understand different points of view, we become transformed by each other's life experiences to a different level of knowledge and sensitive multiethnic care. That's good for children!

Janet Gonzalez-Mena in *Multicultural Issues in Child Care*

In the quote on the preceding page, Janet Gonzalez-Mena is talking about parent-caregiver relationships that support good things happening for children. We think that providers can practice those skills and work on cultivating that same openness with each other in family child care support groups. In this way, providers will be better able to engage parents in the reciprocal relationships Ms. Gonzalez-Mena is talking about. That's good for everyone!

Creating an agenda for the meeting from members' current burning issues and checking in at every meeting allow for this kind of sharing and engagement. Checking in and creating an agenda can be implemented separately. Feel free to initiate them in your support group one at a time. Later you will want to practice them together with agenda items coming from some of the burning issues that members share at check-in.

Check-In at Support Group Meetings

Check-in is a powerful tool for building community and trust in a group. It is practiced from boardrooms to living rooms to farm fields all around the world. Family child care providers check in every day with the parents and children in their groups. They greet each other and briefly share what's happened since the last time they saw each other. Everyone chooses which bits of information are the most important to share at that time. The caregiver welcomes the information, asks questions to be sure she understands fully, and also is careful to limit how long the morning check-in takes.

Check-in at family child care support groups serves a similar purpose but needs to be more structured so that everyone checks in together and the time is shared equally. Check-in serves many important purposes in the life of a group, which is why it should be a part of every meeting. It usually happens near the beginning of each meeting as a way to allow everyone to talk, listen, and connect right away. All members gather in a circle. One by one, each person is given the opportunity to speak uninterrupted for a set amount of time, usually one or two minutes. Anyone who does not want to speak at that time can pass. After everyone has had a turn, those who passed are again offered an opportunity to share. Everything said during check-in is confidential.

Let's look in more detail at some of the important aspects of check-in.

RULES FOR CHECK-IN

- The group sits in a circle, preferably without a table in the middle.

- Each person has a specific amount of time to speak; one or two minutes works best. If the group is large, break into smaller groups or allow thirty seconds for each person.

- The group decides on a focused or unfocused check-in for that meeting.

- One person volunteers to start, and then check-in proceeds either way around the circle from that person.

- A timekeeper uses a timer for each speaker and indicates clearly to the speaker when time is up.

- When time is called, the speaker can very briefly finish the thought she has already started before passing to the next person.

- No conversation, questions, or comments from other members of the group are allowed during or after a person's check-in.

- No one is required to speak. Anyone may pass by just saying, "Pass." At the end of check-in, anyone who passed is offered the opportunity to speak then.

- Everything said during check-in is confidential and is not spoken about outside the room.

- During check-in, an individual can state that she would like some time to address a specific issue with the group later in the meeting. The facilitator or chart writer should add the topic to the agenda. At the end of check-in, the facilitator should ask if anyone else has burning issues to discuss later. These topics should also be written on the group's flip chart agenda.

Check-In Builds Community and Trust

For some members, being listened to so attentively may not happen in any other part of their lives. The act of speaking about whatever is on her mind, not being interrupted, and having others listen without challenging or imposing their own views can have a powerful effect on people, especially on some women. The check-in circle becomes a protected and confidential space where the group honors each individual's experience and feelings in a nonjudgmental way. It gives each person the opportunity to be heard respectfully and to listen carefully to others.

Check-In Can Be Focused or Unfocused

Check-in can be focused or unfocused. During focused check-in, each person speaks on a specific topic that is agreed upon by the whole group beforehand. The topic can be fun or address a more serious issue. Examples: "Tell us about your first car," or "Tell us about changes you're thinking about for your child care space." Focused check-in is often used when a group is just forming, when a new member is joining the group, or to kick off a discussion about a specific topic.

Unfocused check-in, on the other hand, does not address a specific topic. Each person decides what she would like to share with the group that evening. Unfocused check-in is used when a group is well established and members speak openly and trust each other.

Whether using focused or unfocused check-in, the person checking in can state if she would like to discuss a burning issue later in the meeting. The burning issues can be listed on a flip chart, but no other notes or minutes are recorded. Everything stated during check-in is confidential and stays in that room.

Timing Check-In Is Critical

Timing check-in is very important for all members of the group. It is important for the speaker so she can plan her comments according to the time allowed and not ramble on unknowingly and monopolize the group's time. It is important for the listeners because they can relax and pay attention, knowing that they will have exactly the same amount of time as everyone else and that time won't run out before it's their turn. It is important for the timekeeper because she learns to be strong and forthright about enforcing the agreed-upon rules for the group. Timing check-in is a way to share leadership and have all members share the responsibility for the success of each meeting.

HOW LONG IS ONE MINUTE?

It will help your members understand how long they can talk if you show them how long one or two minutes is before they start. Here's one way to do that:

- Ask for a volunteer who doesn't mind talking in front of the group.

- Set your timer for one minute and ask the volunteer to keep talking about her own children (or another nonthreatening topic) until the timer beeps in one minute.

- Say "go" and start your timer. If the volunteer stops talking, motion to her to keep talking until the timer beeps.

- When the timer finally beeps, ask the volunteer and the group how that felt. Usually, people are surprised how much can be said in one minute and feel much more relaxed about having time to say something meaningful in a short time. Without this activity, people tend to rush and stop talking even before their time is up.

Check-In for New Members

At first, check-in can be an intimidating experience. Even those who feel comfortable checking in at their first support group meeting may get home and feel as if they shared too much, sounded silly, or said the "wrong" thing. These are normal feelings that come from the unusual experience of being honest with other adults and being listened to without interruption or sidetracking comments. Here are ways to help new members feel more comfortable with checking in:

1. Explain why check-in is important.

   - Check-in helps members get reconnected every month.

   - Check-in is a time when each member can speak uninterrupted and be listened to respectfully, not giving or taking, just being with the other members of the group in an open way.

- Check-in helps members gain the self-esteem to share their thoughts and feelings with confidence.

- Check-in allows members to identify issues they are facing and may want help with from the group.

2. Plan other community-building activities such as games, a potluck, telephone calls, a retreat, and other go-around activities. Look back at chapter 3 for games and a variety of active check-in suggestions.

3. Acknowledge that creating community is a process and takes time.

4. Remind everyone that she has the option to pass.

5. Propose fun, focused check-in topics when the group is new or members first attend. Here are some examples of fun, focused check-in topics:

   - Tell about your first (choose one) car, job, apartment, etc.

   - If you could be in any other occupation, what would it be?

   - Tell us something we don't know about you.

   - What were your dreams when you were in grade school?

   - What's your favorite (choose one) movie, book, time of day, or month, and why?

   - Give three words that describe your day, week, or year, and explain.

   - Describe a time when you experienced (choose one) prejudice, caring, tenderness, fear, or power.

   - Describe a place that you love.

   - Describe one thing you could teach others and how you learned it.

6. After a focused check-in, ask the group if anyone else has a burning issue she would like to discuss later in the meeting. Write these topics on a flip chart.

Check-In Creates the Meeting Agenda

Check-in is one way the group gathers topics for the meeting's agenda. Each member can state during her check-in time if she would like some time later in the meeting to discuss a current concern, or "burning issue," or any other topic of interest. In this way, check-in helps members learn how to speak up and request the specific support they need from the group. It reminds us that all members have personal and professional challenges, and it acknowledges that our family child care colleagues have wisdom and important experiences to share.

In chapter 11, you'll find a variety of suggestions for ways to approach the topics and issues that the support group members raise. Open discussion is the most common way that most people discuss most things. It works well some of the time, but not always. You will want to learn other ways of structuring your discussions to include more voices and explore more ideas. Talking in pairs, going around the circle, drawing, and writing are some easy and fun alternatives to try with your group. They are all explained in detail in chapter 11.

I had a provider friend whom I was encouraging to come to Sojourn. She knew about check-in and confided to me that she worried about what she would say in front of the group. She worried so much that she wished we didn't have check-in as a part of our meeting. I talked it over with her in order to reassure her about the confidentiality of check-in and the supportive nature of it. She has since come to meetings and now even leads off checking in. She doesn't have any anxiety about it at all now. She and I decided that practicing and getting to know and trust the members is so important in relieving the anxiety of speaking up in the group.

Creating an Agenda at Support Group Meetings

Achieving the objectives of any meeting or training event starts with a well-planned agenda. Attaining the goals for your family child care support group meeting is no different. Even though it may seem straightforward, the "why, who, and how" of setting the agenda should be carefully considered beforehand. If the support group meeting has little structure or if the agenda is ignored, conversation will probably be unfocused and dominated by a few members with strong personalities. If every minute of the meeting is planned with presentations, decision making, and announcements, there will not be time for sharing individual members' current concerns and joys.

We want to be perfectly clear that the informal support and mentoring that goes on in family child care support groups cannot replace formal education. Research clearly shows that providers' participation in higher education raises the quality of care in family child care homes. (Weaver 2002; Kontos 1994). We believe that both formal education and intentional support and mentoring can work together to raise quality and increase longevity.

Why are we having this meeting?

In order to set an agenda, you need to think about "why" this meeting is happening. What are your group's objectives? As you've read in previous chapters, we propose that family child care support groups focus on three objectives:

1. To encourage positive, supportive relationships among the members of the group.

2. To address providers' current concerns at the meetings in order to raise the quality of care for children and improve relationships with the children's families.

3. To build leadership capacity in all the members at every meeting—to support their work with parents, community groups, advocacy in our field, and one another.

We've learned over the years that community-building activities like eating and socializing together, checking in, celebrating together, and going on retreats together help providers become trusted friends and supportive professional colleagues. Allowing time for members to discuss their current burning issues involving individual children, parents, and programming decisions contributes to raising the quality of care in all the members' family child care groups. Sharing leadership among all the members all the time encourages each person to think of herself as a leader in both small and bigger ways—and build her own developmentally appropriate leadership skills, even as she focuses on the challenging job of providing high-quality family child care.

The meeting agenda represents an agreement among group members on how they will spend their time together. The agenda tells the group not only what will be discussed but also what won't be discussed at that meeting. When an agenda is decided months in advance, the group, in effect, is agreeing not to discuss the issues that individual providers are facing on a given evening. If all the meeting time is taken up with presentations, planning, and business, the group is agreeing not to give priority to the day-to-day challenges and decisions that face the providers in the group. If one person takes on the leading and scheduling, the group is agreeing not to support leadership development in all the members.

Your group will probably have its own objectives to add to this list as well. It is important that the members think together about what they want for their meetings and then choose intentional strategies for achieving those goals.

Who decides on the agenda?

In a traditionally run group, the chairperson sets the agenda. This leaves much of the power in the chairperson's hands. When you decide to build the agenda together at each family child care support group meeting, your group is choosing to share that power and encourage members to have input into how you will spend your time together. That's why it's called nonhierarchical or shared leadership.

It's a tall order. How can we create an agenda that is neither too loose nor too tight, have time for socializing and addressing members' current burning issues, and do it all on the spur of the moment? There is an answer, and fortunately, family child care providers who offer high-quality care practice it daily in their family child care programs.

How do we set the agenda together?

Family child care support groups who want to share power and leadership among all their members should create an agenda that is "structured to be flexible." It may sound strange to use both the words "structure" and "flexible" in the same breath, but actually family child care providers already know how to do this.

When you plan your family child care program, it's critical to have a basic structure to the day. The children need the routines of eating, sleeping, and playing outside in roughly the same order and times during the day. This helps children stay healthy and feel secure. At the same time, the schedule needs flexibility to meet the needs of each child and to accommodate special events and those frequent unpredictable teachable moments. One example: an art project you had planned may need to wait until tomorrow because a child arrives wanting to share a cherished storybook.

Likewise, at family child care support group meetings, it's important to have a structure for each meeting so that members feel comfortable and know what to expect. It's also crucial to leave room in the basic structure for immediate concerns and unexpected discussion topics.

Here's the basic family child care support group meeting structure that works for us. We settled on this agenda after trying several variations over the years. We learned to check in before eating so members could address things that came up during that informal socializing period. For example, a provider might follow up on a colleague's check-in by saying, "Your plans for putting in a bathroom next to your child care space sound really exciting. Tell me more about it." We also learned to post announcements in a central location and in the minutes rather than go over them in detail with the group. We prefer to dedicate as much of the meeting as possible to personal interactions and sharing.

Your group will want to adjust this structure for your particular situation, just as each family child care provider settles on a basic structure for the day that works for her and her group.

I belong to another group that does not use a shared leadership format. We try to suppress the need to socialize, but we can't, and therefore the meeting almost always starts ten to twenty minutes late. We often get off track in our discussions, and there is no predicting when the meeting will end. At a Sojourn meeting, I know the meeting will begin after a half hour of socializing time and that we will end promptly at 9:00. By acknowledging and allowing a time for socializing, it makes it easier for the group to stay on track during discussions.

OUR BASIC FAMILY CHILD CARE SUPPORT MEETING STRUCTURE

6:30   Gather at the meeting place, socialize, and visit the provider's child care space.

7:00   Begin the meeting on time by gathering in a circle. Open with a simple ritual like reading a funny or inspirational quote or welcoming a new member. Members volunteer for shared leadership roles for the meeting at this time.

7:10   Check in for one or two minutes per member, depending on how many people are present.

7:40   Break for a light meal and socializing. Some issues that are brought up at check-in are often "solved" during this time as members visit informally and follow up on what was shared during check-in.

8:00   Reconvene and list current concerns or "burning issues" and any short business items on the chart. Decide how much time to spend on each item. Address the agenda items one by one.

8:55   End the meeting with a quick "go-around" to give each member a last chance to share.

9:00   Close on time. The meeting host should announce an end time for members to finish their informal visiting.

Before the meeting starts, the facilitator should write the basic structure for the meeting on a page of the group's flip chart. She leaves a large section open for burning issues and also leaves spaces for the roles that change at each meeting. Before check-in, members sign up to take responsibility for specific roles. During check-in and after eating, burning issues and appropriate time limits for each are added to the chart.

Occasionally, there will be too many burning issues to cover during the time available at the meeting. In those cases, it is critical to decide as a group which ones can be managed well in another way. Maybe a phone call or an e-mail message during naptime the next day will meet one person's needs. Maybe a quick go-around to collect ideas will be exactly what another person needs. The important thing is not to leave someone hanging by running out of time or suggesting that she wait until the next meeting. The provider who brings a burning issue to the group needs help now. By being thoughtful and intentional, you can figure out some way to support her promptly without letting the meeting run over time.

tips

TYPICAL AGENDA

Here is a template for a typical agenda as it would appear on the flip chart at a family child care support group meeting. The times are approximate.

Facilitator   *Adriane*
Process Monitor   *Kay*
Timekeeper   *Natasha*
Note Taker   *Abby*
Chart Writer   *Graciela*
Outreach   *Naomi*
......

7:00	Welcome and roles
7:10	Check-in
7:40	Eat
8:00	Burning issues
	Sarah—Parents paying late
	Vaneska—Biting
	Naomi—Field trips
	Toy exchange
8:55	Go-around
9:00	Close

The Three Basics for Your Support Group

Our group experimented in fits and starts with the many ideas that you are reading about in this book. We did not learn about them in any logical order and we did not implement them all at once. Luckily, we figured out very early that three things are most important for the life and effectiveness of a family child care support group. They are:

- Building trust among your support group members with regular community-building activities

- Checking in at every meeting

- Addressing members' current burning issues at every meeting with a structured and flexible agenda

Even now, fifteen years later, our support group has timed check-in, creates the agenda anew at every meeting, and intentionally eats and plays together regularly. In families, in family child care groups, and in family child care support groups, these activities are at the core of all other important growth and development together.

More Reading

Freire, Paulo. 1970. *Pedagogy of the oppressed.* New York: Continuum Press.

Paulo Freire was a Brazilian educator who offered a dramatic alternative to the common notion of education as something experts give to learners. He suggested that learners take an active role in their education. He empowered learners to identify what they wanted to know and what they needed to get there. His book is short and at times difficult reading, but we couldn't end this chapter without a tip of our hats to Freire's important work on the tremendous power of "non-experts" learning together.

National Congress of Neighborhood Women. 1993. *The neighborhood women's training sourcebook.* Columbia, Md.: The Neighborhood Women's Resource Center. Can be ordered at www.groots.org or call 718-388-8915.

This book is particularly complete in the areas of community building, checking in, honoring differences, expressing appreciation, and taking action. Unfortunately, it's difficult to get. A shorter version of Sourcebook, *called* Empowering Grassroots Leadership, *is available more easily from Imani Family Center, 6350 Garesche Avenue, St. Louis, MO, 63136-3446. 314-381-1915.*

Shaffer, Carolyn R., and Kristen Anundsen. 1993. *Creating community anywhere*. New York: G.P. Putnam's Sons.

This is a general explanation of community processes. Chapters 14, 15, and 16 are especially helpful for getting other ideas about communication, decision making, and addressing conflict in a group.

Five

Inviting a Speaker and Maintaining Support

Create spaces for women learners to talk, question, be in charge,

work together, and succeed.

Jane M. Hugo in *Women as Learners*

Family child care support groups invite speakers to their meetings for a variety of important reasons. Here are some of the main reasons:

- To receive required continuing education hours for cardiopulmonary resuscitation (CPR) and first aid certification; USDA Child and Adult Food Program yearly training; and state licensing renewal requirements

- To stay current with tax, insurance, licensing, certification, and accreditation procedures and rules

- To learn more about child development and subjects pertaining to the care and education offered in the family child care program

- To gain personal inspiration and relaxation

- To receive continuing education credit for the hours they spend at their family child care support groups. Some states only count the hours when an outside trainer is present as credible continuing education hours.

- Some formal training offered outside the support group is inconvenient and inappropriate for family child care providers. In rural areas, formal training opportunities may be held infrequently and involve hours of additional travel time. Classes that are offered to family child care providers are sometimes combined with training for center staff. For subjects like child development and CPR, combining center staff and family child care providers creates excellent opportunities for sharing and getting to know other caregivers. For other topics, however, the realities of life in a family child care home and in a center-based program are different enough to make the combined training less valuable for the family child care providers.

All these reasons help explain why offering formal training at support group meetings remains an important function of many family child care support groups.

Support Group Meetings Offer Much More Than Formal Training

Groups that choose to provide formal training with speakers at their family child care support group meetings should keep these things in mind:

- Providers need time to socialize and maintain their friendships even when a speaker is scheduled.

- Providers will have burning issues that may not be addressed by the speaker. There needs to be time at every meeting for members to check in and make plans for how they will address their current burning issues outside of the meeting time.

- Providers need opportunities to talk with one another after a formal presentation and apply the new ideas to their lives and to their work.

Most experienced adult educators and presenters will structure their presentations to include activities for personal application and different learning styles. They will automatically incorporate discussion and a chance for individuals to critique the material and consider how it applies to them. As we've seen, these considerations are very important because our family child care support group members are primarily adult women who tend to learn best by comparing their knowledge and experience with the new material and with the knowledge and experience of their trusted colleagues. Each member will come to the training at her own level and with her own knowledge and experiences. Through discussion, she can personalize and deepen the knowledge that she constructs for herself.

Providers in my support group came to meetings with different needs, which caused conflict within the group. Some people saw the meeting as a way to meet training requirements and would attend only if there were topics or speakers that were of interest to them. Others in the group wanted social and emotional support and were not getting this when there were speakers. This conflict in direction made attendance spotty and the meetings unsatisfying. This made it difficult for the leader of the group to organize meetings. Trying to find topics and speakers of interest to the group became very time-consuming, especially when the leader was also trying to run her business. All of the responsibility of the success of the meeting fell on the leader.

How to Have a Speaker and Not Give Up the Rest

Your group can take a number of important steps to incorporate a speaker while maintaining your typical meeting format. First, plan time for checking in and socializing before the speaker arrives. Have check-in right away. Then eat and socialize so before the speaker arrives providers can discuss issues that came up during check-in. This also gives them a chance to plan for time outside the meeting to call, e-mail, or get together to address a colleague's burning issue.

If the speaker delivers a lecture, ask that it be no longer than twenty minutes. Be sure to ask if the speaker usually engages the participants in activities and discussion. If so, ask what sorts of activities are used. Don't be afraid to discuss different learning strategies that might be better for your group. This could include individual writing in response to the presentation, talking in pairs or small groups, reacting to scenarios, a question and answer period, or an open discussion with the presenter.

If the presenter doesn't usually involve the audience in discussion or application, you can offer to organize that part. Here are some ways to do that:

- Ask group members to write down their questions at the beginning and end of the presentation. You or the writer could ask the presenter the questions during a Q & A period.

- Divide the large group into smaller groups of three or four and ask people to share stories from their own experience that either affirm or contradict the ideas presented. Give them five to ten minutes for this activity. Ask for volunteers to share at least one story of affirmation and one that seems to contradict the material. Ask the presenter to comment on each story.

- As a summary activity, ask members of the group to share one idea from the presentation that they will want to put into practice right away. You can suggest a quick go-around for this summary. Each member is invited to speak in turn and should keep her comments to one or two sentences. Anyone can pass.

- Follow up on the presentation and the members' engagement with the new material at the next meeting. You could ask, "Does anyone have any thoughts or experiences to share in relation to what the speaker had to say last time?" or "Those of you who put into practice some of the ideas from our last speaker, share with us what happened."

Even if your group members count on the training they receive from speakers at your family child care support group meetings for their continuing education hours, you can still incorporate into every meeting check-in, socializing, and meaningful engagement with the new material. Making check-in a ritual for the beginning of the meeting and practicing attentive timekeeping throughout the meeting will be critical parts of achieving all these goals.

In the future, we hope that state licensing rules will be changed to encourage family child care providers to receive high-quality training in peer mentoring and shared leadership, and to participate in reflective support groups. We believe that excellent peer mentoring and being part of an ongoing community of learners together can raise the quality of care for children in family child care homes (Kontos 1994; Weaver 2002), promote longevity for providers, and build strong leadership capacity within the field of family child care and for our communities.

Checklist of things to consider when planning and to discuss ahead of time with a speaker:

- Come after check-in and snacks.

- Keep the formal presentation to twenty minutes.

- Include opportunities for discussion and activities after the presentation.

- Ask what kinds of activities the presenter has in mind.

- Consider planning the activities and discussion part yourselves.

- Confirm fee or barter arrangements.

- Confirm date, time, and place.

- Ask about any space or equipment needs.

I was the coordinator of our local family child care group for three years. We did contract out for training toward licensing requirements on various topics, but between registration and the training we held a half hour of "get-to-know-you" activities like sharing a comment a child had said that day, how long we'd been licensed, stories about our own kids, what we did before going into child care, where we grew up, etc. Then we tried a "circle time" for providers who had problems they wanted help solving or simply wanted to share. They put questions on a piece of paper or held up a hand if they were comfortable. Then we went around the room and each person gave a short suggestion, the provider said "thank you," and the next suggestion came. Someone recorded this for the provider to read at home and try out. We realized that there was training going on by sharing with one another in these formal and informal ways.

More Reading

Hayes, Elisabeth, and Daniele Flannery, with Ann K. Brooks, Elizabeth J. Tisdell, and Jane M. Hugo. 2000. *Women as learners: The significance of gender in adult learning.* San Francisco: Jossey-Bass.

Because so many family child care providers are women, we believe that we have an obligation to apply current knowledge and understanding about women as learners when planning family child care training, mentoring programs, support groups, and educational programming. This collection of papers by Hayes, Flannery, Brooks, Tisdell, and Hugo gives an excellent overview of what we know about adult women as learners. The chapters are short and understandable with the added benefit of the authors' research to back them up.

Six

Making Decisions Together

Our experience has been that a group that takes itself seriously
must develop its own structures for meetings. . . . If not, we have
found that women are left to the mercies of group members'
feelings, personal agendas, and socially-conditioned roles in
society. Too many meetings are either chaotic or overly controlled.

From *The Neighborhood Women's Training Sourcebook*

There are two sets of agreements that a family child care support group will want to make early on in order to encourage shared vision, full participation, and a comfortable meeting. The two sets of agreements are:

- Logistical decisions about meeting place, day, time, food, attendance, facilitator, and dues

- Group guidelines for communication and interaction

It will be up to your group to decide which set of agreements it makes sense to start with. If your group is newly forming, you may need to agree on where and when to meet before anything else can happen. Groups who are already meeting can go ahead and set group guidelines but may want to revisit logistics for the meeting as a way to explore these decision-making strategies.

Considerations about Meeting Logistics

One set of agreements your family child care support group will need to make has to do with the logistics of the meetings—the location, day, time, refreshments, finances, attendance, child care, and facilitator. These decisions need to be made pretty quickly in the life of the group, but they can be changed if the initial decision isn't working well for one reason or another.

Let's look at some of the things you may want to consider about each one:

Location of the Meeting

Some groups prefer meeting in a public place like a library, school, or church. Others prefer meeting in homes where they can see and learn from each other's child care spaces. It is our experience that newer providers tend to feel more comfortable starting out in a public place. If you decide to meet in homes, be sure to publicize where the meeting will be held, take extra pains to give directions or a ride to new members, and welcome them warmly. When there are only two choices for places to meet, be sure to encourage discussion on both choices. If a show of hands reveals that both options are equally popular, explore whether there is a way to combine the two or try one for a while and then try the other. When you have several options, multi-voting would probably work well for deciding where to have the family child care support group meetings. Multi-voting is described later in this chapter—see page 63.

Day for the Meeting

Most family child care support groups meet once a month. Ours does, too, and that schedule has served us well for fifteen years. Meeting more often over the long run does not seem to increase attendance. That said, we strongly suggest choosing a specific day of a specific week within the month that does not change. For example: The group could decide to meet on the second Wednesday evening of each month. This allows members to give priority to their family child care support group meeting and put it on their calendars for the entire year. Meeting on a predictable day at a predictable time also makes it easier for new members to attend.

If your members have commitments that conflict with that one day, the group can consider alternating between two days in the same week. For example: One month, the meeting could be on the second Wednesday and the next month, the meeting could be on the second Thursday. We have found that alternating between more than two dates, for example, one month on Monday, the next on Tuesday, next on Wednesday, and then on Thursday, does not increase attendance. It just confuses everyone. Even alternating between two days does not guarantee that the people for whom the group is alternating will come to the meetings. Those members are clearly very busy and will miss meetings anyway. At least by alternating days, the group allows for the possibility that all members can come to some of the meetings.

Discussion and a show of hands will often work for deciding the meeting day. If you do have several options, use multi-voting (see page 63) to figure out the best one for your group as a whole.

Length of Time for the Meeting

Out of respect for members' family and work responsibilities, it's very important to start and end the formal part of your support group meeting on time. Be careful to plan your meeting times carefully so that you can accomplish that comfortably.

We've found that two to two and one-half hours works well for the length of our meetings. We started with two-hour meetings, but that was not enough time to visit and reconnect with each other. We ended up adding a half hour to the beginning, before the meeting formally starts, for informal socializing. This also gives our members more leeway for when they arrive. If they want to socialize and look at the meeting host's child care space, they come early. If they have other responsibilities or only want to attend the formal support group meeting, they come a half hour later. Since we include fifteen to twenty minutes of eating and socializing during the meeting as well, no one completely misses out on informal socializing and building community. Discussion and a show of hands will probably suffice for deciding this issue.

Food at the Meeting

Eating together and socializing around food should be an important component of your family child care support group meeting. Some groups like to have the meeting host provide the food. Others prefer potluck. Some groups have a couple of people share the responsibility of bringing food to each meeting. For some groups a snack is perfect, and for others a light meal is more appropriate because some members do not have time to eat dinner before they arrive. Each group will need to choose the best solution depending on their meeting time and meeting place. Be sure to consider any food restrictions of your members. Some may be vegetarian or have specific allergies or food requirements. All group members should have this information so that everyone can enjoy the food together.

We'd suggest using the multi-voting process to decide this issue; see page 63.

Attendance at the Meetings

In most groups, there are no expectations about attendance, and people come or don't come whenever they want. There are some groups, however, that expect members to come to all meetings.

In groups where attendance is expected, they communicate that expectation when new members inquire about joining. Sometimes a new member is ready for that commitment. At other times, the prospective member decides that she can't make that promise to the group immediately because of other responsibilities. A year later, when she is more available, she may decide to join the group as a committed member. If your group wants to encourage its members to form a cohesive and supportive community with and for each other, they should consider expecting members to attend every meeting or adopt a variation on that idea.

In our group, we ask for a commitment to attend meetings and check in with each other every year about how that is working out. Naturally, it's understood that people will miss meetings from time to time. Our guideline is that it be no more than two times per year.

People often ask us if we require members to leave the group if they do not attend regularly. We don't. By reminding ourselves of this expectation on a yearly basis, members usually make the appropriate decision for themselves. Members who know that they will be very busy for a while tell the group about the possibility of being absent more often. Naturally, we are delighted to see them whenever they can get to the meeting and keep in touch by phone when they can't make it.

Since all members are expected at every meeting, we also ask that people call the meeting host if they are going to be late or absent. That way no one worries and we can take action if the person needs some special support.

Since this may be a more controversial decision, we suggest that your group decide this issue by using a technique called "gradients of agreement." How to use a Gradients of Agreement Scale is described later in the chapter—see page 65.

Child Care During Meetings

For some providers, it will be impossible to attend support group meetings if they cannot bring their children along. Providing child care at the support group location will be very important if your group has such a member or wants to encourage those providers to attend. If you decide to provide child care, you will need to plan for an appropriate environment, equipment and toys, responsible caregivers/babysitters, snacks, payment for the caregivers, and clean-up! Many family child care providers value their support group meetings as a time with adults and away from children. Making sure that the child care arrangement works smoothly and that the children are safe and happy will go a long way toward meeting everyone's needs.

Your group may also want to talk about infants accompanying their moms to meetings and any guidelines for that situation. These topics will probably generate a lot of discussion. You will want to use the Gradients of Agreement Scale, multi-voting, and a final go-around to make sure everyone shares her ideas.

Financing the Group

Most groups collect minimal dues to cover copying and mailing costs, cards and presents, and sometimes membership fees to professional organizations. When a group invites speakers, it will probably be paying them an honorarium. Fundraising, obtaining grants, or soliciting donations may be necessary to cover those expenses. Your group will need to decide which system for raising money works best for you. In either case, one member should be in charge of collecting the money, keeping the accounts, and writing the checks for a specific length of time, usually a year or two.

Discussion and a show of hands may work well for deciding this issue. If it becomes more controversial, using a combination of multi-voting (page 63) and the Gradients of Agreement Scale (page 65) would work well.

Choosing a Facilitator

Your group may have a person or small group that is already leading the transition to some of these shared leadership practices. It is perfectly all right to continue with that person or group in this leadership role for the time being. When your group is ready to formally choose a group facilitator, you will want to read the section in chapter 8 about basic shared leadership roles and, specifically, the role of facilitator. One method for choosing the facilitator is called "Tapped-on-the-Shoulder." This method follows:

activity

TAPPED-ON-THE-SHOULDER

You may be ready to choose a facilitator for the group. Tapped-on-the-Shoulder is an easy way to choose the facilitator as you get started with shared leadership. It can also be used for other roles your group decides to use.

Materials you'll need for Tapped-on-the-Shoulder: paper and pens.

How to proceed:
- Ask all the members to write down, in order of preference, two people they think would make a good facilitator for the group and would benefit from the leadership experience.

- One or two people are designated as vote counters. They collect the papers and take them home.

- Absent members are asked to send/take/e-mail their choices for facilitator to the vote counters, who then count all the results.

- The person with the most votes, whether she is first or second choice, is asked to be the facilitator. If there is a tie, the person with the most first-choice votes is asked to be the facilitator. If the first person asked declines, the next person is asked to fill the role for the group.

- This method can be used again the next time you change facilitators, asking that past facilitators not be considered for the leadership position.

Basic Decision-Making Strategies

Multi-Voting

Here's an example of how to make decisions using a more-inclusive voting system than the usual yes/no or either/or type of vote. It is called multi-voting because each person can vote for more than one option. This system allows the decision making to include members' second and third choices and increases the chances that the group will come up with a solution that is agreeable with and has buy-in from everyone.

In an election where the majority wins, almost half of the members could be disappointed because their choice lost. With multi-voting, the winning vote-getter is a mixture of first-, second-, and third-choice votes, which brings many more members into the group that voted for the "winner."

activity

MULTI-VOTING

Multi-voting is an excellent technique to use when there are many possible solutions to choose from. Materials you'll need for multi-voting: flip chart, markers, colored sticky dots, and pens. Here's how to practice multi-voting:

- Brainstorm possible solutions with the whole group and write them all down in a list on the flip chart. All ideas are welcome. Don't take time to judge or discuss at this point.

- Group similar ideas and eliminate repetitions with permission from the people who made those suggestions.

- Invite discussion on the items that are left.

- If there are lots of choices, have each member write down her top five and eliminate the ones that no one picked.

- Highlight the choices that are left or rewrite them for clarity.

- Pass out colored sticky dots to each member. One rule of thumb is to give each member one dot for every three choices on the list. For example: If your group has come up with nine possible ways to get food to the meeting, each person will get three sticky dots to vote for their top three choices.

- Before asking members to get up and vote, give them a chance to think and to decide. Have them also write the number three on one dot, two on the next dot, and one on the last dot.

- All members get up at the same time and cast their votes by sticking the number three dot next to their *first* choice, the number two dot next to their *second* choice, and the number one dot next to their *third* choice. We know this sounds counter-intuitive, but give it a try. It works!

- Once everyone has placed her dots on the list, you can either simply count the dots or add up the point value next to each choice. The "winner" is the item with the most dots or the most points—your choice. If there is a tie, the one with the most first choices (or number three dots) wins.

- Go around the group for individual reactions to the outcome of the vote.

- Adjust the plan if necessary. Even after a "vote," you may still find the solution isn't quite meeting everyone's needs. In that case, you can redo the process with new and improved options.

During my time as the facilitator of Sojourn, we worked toward choosing a new name (we were originally called The Senior Providers). Choosing a new name for the group was a lengthy process and I had to remind myself that the process was more important than getting to a quick solution. Our group tried the strategy of multi-voting for the first time while trying to choose a new name. We also made drawings that represented what the group meant to each of us. In order to make sure that everyone had a say, the process had to take as long as it was going to take. It sounds funny because we use a timekeeper, but we really had to let go of time in order to let this process take place with input from everyone in the group. Everyone's voice counts!

GRADIENTS OF AGREEMENT SCALE—adapted from *Facilitator's Guide to Participatory Decision Making* (1996) by Kaner, Lind, Toldi, Fisk, and Berger

Using a Gradients of Agreement Scale, the group can check out more specifically how people feel about a proposal before they formally adopt it. The Gradients of Agreement Scale is a very helpful tool when making a controversial decision that will need the group's enthusiastic support to succeed, or when there are only two choices to pick from.

Materials you'll need for using a Gradients of Agreement Scale: flip chart, markers, and sticky dots.

How to use the Gradients of Agreement Scale in making decisions:
• When the top choice has been identified by a show of hands or multi-voting, show the group this Gradients of Agreement Scale written on a piece of flip chart paper:

Agree	Agree with reservations	Don't care	Don't like it but I can live with it	Disagree	Refuse to accept this (Block)

- Go around the circle, asking each person to briefly tell which gradient best describes her support or lack of support for the top proposal and why. For example, a member might say, "At this point, I would pick 'Agree with reservations' because . . ." This allows members to hear each other's thinking before actually voting.

- After the go-around, ask for a show of hands for each step of the Gradients of Agreement Scale and write the number of votes for each step on the chart. You could also use sticky dots for this step.

- Ask the people who voted "Don't care," or "Don't like," or "Disagree" what could be changed in the proposal to make it more acceptable to them. Invite discussion on those ideas. See if the group can come up with a new proposal incorporating those ideas.

- Using the Gradients of Agreement Scale, poll the group again about the new proposal and write down the votes on the chart.

- Ask if the group feels like the new proposal has enough support to go ahead. If so, state the group's new proposal and have a go-around to get everyone's feelings about the decision.

- If the group decides that there is not enough support, suggest taking the discussion up again at the next meeting.

- Have a go-around to hear everyone's feelings about the process and the outcome so far.

At the next meeting, you can ask for any thoughts that came up over the past month about this issue and suggest that the group pick up again with brainstorming and discussing. The group may decide to form an ad hoc committee to discuss alternatives and present them to the group at a later meeting.

The process of struggling together, learning and practicing some new decision-making techniques, and finally reaching a decision that is acceptable to all members can give the group a tremendous sense of trust, solidarity, and satisfaction. It is worth being patient and committing the time to make sure that the process is respectful and inclusive to all.

Choosing Group Communication and Interaction Guidelines

Every person comes to the group with patterns and norms of communication that she brings from her own family and culture. Some of those expectations have to do with class, race, ethnic origin, and gender, while others may have to do with personality, education, first language, age, past experiences, and even birth order. Some of your group members may have similar expectations about how people "should" behave in groups and in conversations while others expect something altogether different.

Discussing and agreeing on ground rules for communication in your support group clears the way for all members to participate confidently and with sensitivity. When interactions or communication among members begins to disintegrate, written group guidelines allow anyone in the group to quickly remind others of the rules and get back on track.

Coming up with group guidelines does not need to take a long time. Here's one way to do it; you will need these materials: paper, pencils, a hat, several pieces of large chart paper, markers, and tape.

- Pass out identical pieces of paper and pencils to all members. Ask everyone in the group to spread out around the room. Tell them to write the number one on one side of the paper and the number two on the other.

- On the first side, each member should write down the things about group discussion and just being in a group that are difficult for her. On the other side, have them write the things they like to find in interactions with friends and colleagues. Tell them that their ideas will remain anonymous. Someone else will read their ideas to the group. The papers should be folded, put into the hat, and shuffled.

- One by one, each member chooses a piece of paper from the hat and reads both sides aloud. Another member writes down the statements on the flip chart in a way that creates a guideline for the group.

For example:

- If a person wrote, "It is really irritating to have one person talk for a long time," the guideline might read, "Keep your comments brief."

- If a person wrote, "I keep quiet because some people gossip after the meetings," the guideline might read, "Everything said at the meeting will be kept strictly confidential and will not be spoken about later to anyone except with the permission of the speaker."

- As you go along, some comments may be repeated. You do not need to write those again. Instead put a star by the original item to show that it was mentioned more than once.

- After all the ideas have been noted, ask for feedback. Are there any guidelines you don't understand? Are there any that you don't agree with? Are there any that can be combined? Are each person's ideas still there? Did you think of any others in the meantime?

- Ask for any last comments from the group as a whole. Then go around the group one by one so that each person can share her personal feelings about the group guidelines.

- Before the next meeting, write down the final guidelines. They can be posted at the meetings or brought out at strategic times. The group can revisit them occasionally to see if they still fit or if changes are necessary.

Above all, be patient and take your time. Making good decisions together creates trust and openness that will support all the other work of the group. When members feel safe and that their ideas are valued, they are more likely to want to be at the meetings and to participate fully.

tips

Here is a common list of guidelines. After your group comes up with its list, you can share this one with group members and see if they want to add any of these to their list.

- Listen carefully with full attention.

- Speak honestly using "I" statements.

- Encourage everyone to speak. Respect the right of everyone to pass.

- Speak positively about ourselves and others.

- Separate people from issues. Express opinions on issues and be gentle on people.

- Be welcoming to different approaches and don't let one cultural or religious view dominate.

- Give advice only when specifically asked.

- Avoid side comments and interruptions.

- Take responsibility to get your own needs met.

- Bring a balance of personal and professional issues to the group.

- Respect time and format guidelines and try to give everyone equal time.

- Keep everything shared at the meeting confidential.

More Reading

National Congress of Neighborhood Women. 1993. *The neighborhood women's training sourcebook.* Columbia, Md.: The Neighborhood Women's Resource Center.

This book is hard to obtain, but it is well worth trying. Their treatment of creating group guidelines, addressing diversity issues, and empowering local women is especially powerful. Look for it at www.groots.org or call 718-388-8915 to order a copy.

WomanSpirit. 2003. *Empowering grassroots leadership.* Circles of Hope, Imani Family Center, 6350 Garesche Avenue, St. Louis, MO 63136-3446. 314-381-1915.

This inspiring addition to the literature about how to implement shared leadership and take action in your community is short, friendly, and easy to read, and it has great illustrations. The material is based on The Neighborhood Women's Training Sourcebook *so it is an excellent way to get an introduction to their work and to get your friends and neighbors working together.*

Seven

Practicing Facilitative Skills

There are a great many groups whose members genuinely want each other to voice their opinions, share their insights, and come up with interesting new ideas. But the range and the richness of their discussion will be limited by the degree to which they can tolerate diverse communication styles. . . . Using good facilitative skills can be an excellent support to such groups.

Sam Kaner, Lenny Lind, Catherine Toldi, Sarah Fisk, and Duane Berger in *Facilitator's Guide to Participatory Decision Making*

In groups where all members take responsibility for positive interactions and the success of the meetings, it is very helpful if everyone has some basic facilitation skills. These are not complicated skills that necessitate specialized training. These are strategies that many people use naturally in the normal course of everyday life. By giving these skills a name and understanding the function they serve in relationships, all members of shared leadership groups can be more intentional about choosing and implementing appropriate facilitation tools in any situation.

Facilitative skills create interactions that help members do the following:

- Participate more fully in discussion

- Think about things from a variety of viewpoints

- Gather more information about their situation

- Express important feelings

- Consider how others' experiences relate to their own

- Gain clarity about conflict and possible next steps

- Find strategies to improve the quality of care they provide

- Gain experience with skills that will improve conversations with parents

Facilitative skills encourage all members to take these steps toward making room for everyone:

- Respect one another's differences, whatever shape they take

- Create community and trust with each other

- Listen more carefully

- Be honest and compassionate

- Ask intentional questions

- Refrain from giving advice

- Support each other exactly where they are

- Challenge each other to take the next step

High-quality family child care providers are constantly making intentional choices about how to interact with a specific child in a given situation. In reality, they are choosing the specific facilitative strategies that are most likely to support that child's development and learning.

They can put these same facilitative strategies to use with their family child care colleagues, with the children's parents, and with other adults. When applying these concepts to interactions with adults, we give the strategies specific names and describe the differences between them, but basically, they are the same skills that high-quality caregivers use moment to moment with children.

Facilitative Strategies That All Group Members Should Use

Here are some basic facilitative strategies with examples from everyday life in a family child care home. Both the facilitator of the group and all of the group members will want to use these skills regularly in their support group meetings. We adapted many of these strategies for family child care providers from *Facilitator's Guide to Participatory Decision Making* (1996) by Kaner, Lind, Toldi, Fisk, and Berger.

HELPFUL FACILITATIVE STRATEGIES FOR GROUP MEMBERS

1. Paraphrasing

2. Drawing Out

3. Encouraging

4. Balancing

5. Making Space

6. Gathering Ideas

7. Refraining from Giving Advice

Paraphrasing

Maya, a four-year-old, sobs as she tells her provider how two other four-year-olds are being mean, keeping all the good markers to themselves, leaving her out of the game, and saying that her picture is not pretty. The provider puts her arm around the child and says, "I can tell that you're very sad about this. It sounds like the other kids are forgetting to share and they even said a rough thing about your drawing."

This is an example of paraphrasing. The provider is using her own words to say what she hears the child expressing. Paraphrasing tends to have a calming and clarifying effect on both children and adults. It reassures the speaker that we have been listening carefully and that we understand what she said. Here are some examples of how paraphrasing with adults starts:

- "Let me see if I understand . . ."

- "So, what you're saying is . . ."

- "This is what I'm hearing . . ."

Drawing Out

Anthony, a seven-year-old, arrives at the provider's home after taking the bus from school. Anthony says, "There were some big kids on the bus." The provider answers, "Big kids? Hmmm. Tell me what happened."

In this example, the provider used paraphrasing first to let the child know that she was listening ("Big kids? Hmmm.") and then she used the technique called drawing out to encourage the child to tell her more. Paraphrasing and drawing out are most effectively used together with adults as well. Many adults like to know that the listener understands them first before they are willing to reveal more. Asking open-ended questions is the best way to encourage people to clarify and refine their ideas. Questions with yes or no answers are not as helpful. Drawing out your fellow family child care support group members and other adults might sound like this:

- "Can you say more about that?"

- "Could you give us an example?"

- "Help me out with that. You are against that solution because . . ."

Encouraging

The children have just returned after the July 4th weekend. They are bursting with news about fireworks, picnics, trips, and family gatherings. The provider says, "I want to hear about everyone's holiday. Natasha went to see the fireworks. Did anyone else watch fireworks?"

Encouraging is the way we inspire people to stay engaged without singling out any one person. With children, we often encourage with our tone of voice, with our body language, and by planning activities that we know the children will enjoy. We can do some of that with adults, but more often, encouraging takes the form of compelling questions, addressing relevant topics in discussion, and formats for the discussion that encourage full participation like talking in pairs or using go-arounds. Examples of encouraging comments we might say to the adults in our family child care support groups are as follows:

- "Several long-term providers have given their perspective. Let's hear from newer providers."

- "Who else has an idea?"

- "Does anyone have an example of that?"

Balancing

Samantha, a three-year-old, runs over to her provider saying that Jiho, another three-year-old, took the blanket she was using. The provider says, "Oh, dear. He took your blanket. That's a problem." (Paraphrasing.) "Tell me what happened." (Drawing out.) After Samantha finishes her version, the provider, knowing there are always two sides to the story, says, "Let's go talk with Jiho and see what he has to say. Jiho, Samantha says . . . tell me about the blanket."

This provider knows that even though she has no idea what Jiho's version of the story might be, she needs to get his side before going any further. She is practicing balancing. She is requiring Samantha to join her in rounding out the discussion with more points of view. She is telling them both that everyone's view is important and that it's safe and okay to acknowledge the conflict and keep talking.

Oh, yes. Conflict. Seeking out different points of view and finding balance in issues between children will be much easier for most of us than inviting and searching out balance in issues facing adults. We tend to be much less bold in inviting and respecting differences of opinion between adults. Nevertheless, being able to openly and respectfully address differences with parents, colleagues, and policy makers is a critical leadership skill that everyone in the group can practice. In *Multicultural Issues in Child Care*, Janet Gonzalez-Mena tells us, "As early childhood educators, we need much more training on how to react to conflict. We need to learn how to put judgment aside and start a dialog based on respect and a willingness to listen."

Here are some ways that you can invite balance into a discussion in your family child care support group:

- "OK, now we know how two people stand on this subject. Who has a different opinion?"

- "Are there other ways of looking at this?"

- "This is a controversial topic. Let's start out with a poll. How many of you think . . ."

Making Space

Victor, an eighteen-month-old, babbles away at the lunch table, raises his voice, and bangs his spoon. His provider says, "I think Victor wants to be part of the conversation too. Let's listen to what he has to say. Victor, tell us about that yummy apple."

In this example, the provider is making space for the younger child to share and join in the discussion around the lunch table. With adults, the technique of making space helps quiet members and newer members participate fully. Examples of things you might say when making space with adults are as follows:

- "Lots of people have comments. Let's raise hands so everyone gets a chance to speak."

- "Usha, it seems like you might want to add something."

- "Mare, I'm curious what you are thinking about this."

- "Let's go around the circle and get everyone's initial comments on this topic."

Gathering Ideas

Food is getting low in the house. The provider gets out a piece of paper at breakfast and says, "I am going shopping for groceries this evening and I would like you to help me with the shopping list. I might not be able to buy all of your suggestions, but I will definitely buy some of them. Russell, tell me one thing that you would like to eat for lunch next week." The provider proceeds to write down each child's suggestion.

The provider in this example was using the technique of gathering ideas. She gave a precise description of the task and limited the amount that each child could contribute. She honored each suggestion by writing it down and made space for all to give their ideas. Gathering ideas—closely related to brainstorming—is no different with adults. In your family child care support group, you might use this technique in these ways:

- "Let's generate a list of ideas on this topic. We won't discuss them now. Let's just get a lot of ideas up here to get started."

- "Let's make two lists, one of the pros and the other of the cons of this idea as you see it. We won't discuss them as we go along. Just call them out. First a pro and then a con."

I was asked to facilitate at a conference for Jewish educators within my community. The meeting was filled with professors and adult educators, but I felt I could do well at this task because I had recently been the facilitator for Sojourn for two years. The group at the meeting comprised fifteen people, including a rabbi, and early-childhood teachers and directors. Although I didn't know the subject matter ahead of time, I relied on the tools I learned while leading the support group. I asked questions to clarify points and to help people draw out their thoughts more completely. I made sure everyone had a chance to speak. I used brainstorming as a device for us to share what resources are available in our community. I had a fantastic response to my facilitation once the meeting was over, both verbally and within the written evaluations of the conference. More important, I knew I had learned much from my experiences at my family child care support group that would translate well into any group meeting situation.

Refraining from Giving Advice

Three-year-olds Kenton and Susanna are building with cardboard blocks. They have built a tower as high as they can and Susanna is on tiptoes trying to put on another block. The tower is teetering. The provider says, "What a tall tower! It looks like it's almost going to fall, Susanna. Did you want it to go higher?" The children nod yes. The provider says, "How could we get the block up there without making the tower fall down?"

Susanna says, "You put it up there."

The provider says, "Good thinking. Okay, let's see if that works. Did it?"

"Yes!" say the children as they get another block.

The provider says, "Now how could you get way up here to put on the block yourself?" Kenton says, "Lift me up."

The provider says, "Another good idea! Let's try it. Did it work?"

"Yes!" And the children get another block.

The provider challenges them further. "Let's think some more. How could you get up this high without my lifting you?"

Naturally, older children are paying attention by this time and one of them says, "Get a stool." The provider looks at Kenton and Susanna and asks, "What do you think of that idea?" They nod and run off to get a stool.

The provider in the previous example didn't give advice. By staying engaged with the children and asking them open-ended questions, she helped the children think for themselves. When the older children did give advice, the provider showed respect for the young builders by asking if that suggestion worked for them. Family child care providers are in the business of human development and appropriate teaching and learning. As this example illustrates, providers who offer high-quality care scaffold children's learning and encourage their emotional, social, physical, and cognitive development in appropriate ways all day long. They completely understand the concept of refraining from giving advice when it comes to children's development.

When it comes to understanding adult development and giving advice to other providers, family child care providers join ranks with most other people. Providers, like most adults, often feel free to go ahead and offer each other specific advice right away. Naturally, adults have a lot of experience and knowledge to offer each other, so why keep quiet when we could just tell the other person what works best?

Giving advice may be perfectly appropriate in some situations. In family child care support groups, however, we suggest that providers refrain from giving advice right away. No one else knows all the details of another provider's situation. What worked in one situation may not be appropriate in a similar (but not exactly the same) situation. No one else knows what each individual provider might be struggling with personally and what her next step of personal or professional development is going to be. The only person who can take into consideration the constellation of details and people in a given situation, come up with a feasible solution, and figure out the way she can or can't implement it is the provider herself.

Basic Strategies in Supporting a Colleague to Do Her Best Thinking

There are three basic ways to help a colleague sort through an issue and to come up with a solution that will work for her.

- Listen attentively and use facilitative skills to help her do her best thinking.

- Ask open-ended questions and offer alternative formats for discussion. For example: writing and talking in pairs

- Tell stories from experience.

Listening to a provider speak about a concern and then engaging her in an open-ended way gives her lots of room to choose her own direction for thinking and acting. Here are some examples of open-ended questions:

- How does the time of day affect the situation?

- How does the environment affect the child's behavior?

- What do you notice in the parent-child relationship that may be related?

- How does your behavior make the situation better or worse?

- For you to be happy with the situation, what would need to be different?

- What is in the way of that happening?

- What are your options?

- If you had to pick one thing that you are afraid of, what would it be?

- How can we help you?

Other strategies to help the provider do her best thinking:

- Listen, be present and quietly supportive.

- Use the facilitative skills listed above. (For example, "Tell me more about that.")

- Challenge and encourage when appropriate. (For example, "I remember that you spoke up that other time. What's different this time?")

- Share your own experiences by using "I" statements and telling stories about yourself.

- Be careful not to give your own opinion veiled as a question. (For example, "Don't you think that . . .?")

- Go slowly, patiently, and respectfully with the person seeking help. It may have been very difficult to expose herself to the group in this way and ask for help.

It is best to wait until the provider has done a lot of her own thinking and asks to hear about others' experiences. At the end of a discussion, it would also be possible for the group to ask for her permission to share a few of their experiences. For example, "Would you like to hear some of our experiences with that issue? They aren't exactly the same, but they might give you some more things to think about," or "Once, I was working with a family that . . . here's what we did in that situation . . . ," or "I recently read an article in *Young Children* that talked about that issue. Would you like me to get you a copy?" It is important to have someone take notes or to chart these suggestions so the provider has a list of suggestions to take home and doesn't have to take notes as she listens, thinks, and answers.

As we've seen, family child care providers who offer high-quality care are experts at facilitating thinking, growth, and development in children. By working together, providers can apply these same strategies to support thinking, decision making, growth, and development among their family child care colleagues. In addition, knowing how and when to use these valuable facilitative skills with adults builds leadership capacity that providers can take with them as they work with parents or with any other group in their community.

More Reading

Kaner, Sam, Lenny Lind, Catherine Toldi, Sarah Fisk, and Duane Berger. 1996. *Facilitator's guide to participatory decision making.* Philadelphia: New Society Publishers.

Kaner, Lind, Toldi, Fisk, and Berger's guidebook is easy to read and understand and has excellent information for small facilitative groups. It is especially helpful because many of the pages are laid out as a handout so you can share them one by one with your support group. Kaner's organization, Community at Work, gives permission to people to copy their materials for educational purposes. If you are going to buy one other book to support your group in the implementation of facilitation, participatory processes, and decision making, this is the one to buy.

Green, Tova, and Peter Woodrow with Fran Peavey. 1994. *Insight and action: How to discover and support a life of integrity and commitment to change.* Philadelphia: New Society Publishers.

This is a short, easy-to-read book on small-group process that includes suggestions for "clearing" sessions for individuals. The section on strategic questioning is particularly insightful and complete.

Eight

Understanding the Basic Roles
Facilitator, Timekeeper, Meeting Host, Group Member

Share power. Although some see empowerment as threatening, in reality, empowerment creates new forms of power. Some teachers and caregivers fear that empowerment means giving away their own power, but this is not true! No one can give personal power, and no one can take it away. We all have our personal power, though we can be discouraged or prevented from recognizing or using it. Sharing power, or empowerment, enhances everyone's power.

Janet Gonzalez-Mena in *Multicultural Issues in Child Care*

The enormous difference between hierarchical or directive leadership and shared leadership can be summed up in one word—responsibility. In directive or hierarchical leadership, we give ultimate responsibility and power to the leader for the success or failure of the effort. The leader may delegate tasks to others but retains most of the power and responsibility to organize, follow up, and motivate others.

Directive leadership is a very useful type of leadership at times. It is crucial for getting new ideas off the ground. Those of you reading this book will need to use some enthusiastic directive leadership to encourage your group to try out some of the ideas presented here. You'll need to lead them in a sensitive and directive way in learning about the concepts and strategies of shared leadership. Little by little, as the group develops trust, community, and experience with shared leadership, your charismatic and directive approach will no longer be needed. They will become a group of leaders empowering each other and sharing power.

Shared leadership is another very important type of leadership. Like facilitative leadership, it is not authoritarian; it focuses on the strengths of individuals and seeks to develop leadership capacity in everyone (Sullivan 2002). In a group practicing shared leadership, everyone in the group has the power and responsibility all the time for supporting individuals in the group and facilitating the group's process. Some members agree to perform specific assigned responsibilities or roles, but even that does not leave them alone with the responsibility. Any member of the group can and should respectfully share her opinion, offer suggestions, or volunteer support at appropriate times.

As we've emphasized before, building community and trust among the family child care support group members at every meeting is critical to successful shared leadership. Group structures that encourage open communication need to be in place. Members cannot be expected to voice their opinions and feelings candidly if they do not feel invited, accepted, connected, and safe. If a member is uncomfortable with something that is happening in the group, it is very important that she be able to share her concerns with the group. Shared leadership means being responsible and engaged oneself and seeking out the full engagement of others.

In this chapter, we will look at four different roles that all members can take on immediately as your group learns to share leadership. Here they are:

- Facilitator

- Timekeeper

- Meeting Host
- Group Member

Fundamental Roles Used in Shared Leadership

At first, the facilitator and timekeeper roles should be filled by members who are willing to learn the skills that will allow them to be effective role models for the group. To help members begin to understand what it means to share leadership, you can read and discuss some of the chapters of this book together. Also, playing some of the leadership games in chapter 3 and reflecting on those experiences is another active and fun way to learn about each other and the process of shared leadership together.

Facilitator

Facilitators serve the group in two very distinct ways:

- FACILITATORS MANAGE THE GROUP'S PROCESS.

The facilitator helps the group honor the guidelines and process that they have agreed to follow during their support group meetings. For example, the facilitator makes sure to start the meeting on time. We suggest that the group's facilitator hold this part of the role for one to two years. Our experience shows that it takes a while to learn and practice the skills a person needs for planning a meeting, using alternative discussion formats, dealing with conflict, making participatory decisions, etc.

- FACILITATORS HELP ALL GROUP MEMBERS DO THEIR BEST THINKING, SPEAKING, AND LISTENING DURING A DISCUSSION.

The facilitator of a discussion listens, asks questions, and can be in charge of who talks when. She uses many of the facilitative skills that you read about in chapter 7. She does not take part in the discussion herself. When the group facilitator wants to take part in the discussion, someone else will need to step up to assume the facilitation role for that discussion.

When we first started using shared leadership and participatory strategies in our family child care support group, the group facilitator filled both of these parts of the role nearly all the time. Now, because so many of our members are skilled in facilitating discussion, the official group facilitator takes care of the first part of this role, managing the group's process, and the other group members spontaneously volunteer to facilitate individual discussions.

In community groups that are not familiar with shared leadership, the facilitator will usually be responsible for both of these parts, so we suggest that support group members intentionally learn how to manage them both at the same time. An alternative to merging these two parts of the facilitator's role would be to divide them more clearly. One person could be responsible for the first part—managing the group's process—and be called the "meeting convener or organizer." A small team of members could take the second part—helping members do their best thinking—and be called "discussion facilitators."

The facilitator helps guide group process by taking care of these tasks:

- Making sure the chart paper, easel, markers, and timer are at the meeting

- Setting up a place for announcements

- Posting the agenda template

- Inviting people to be timekeeper, chart writer, etc., for the meeting

- Starting and ending the meeting on time

- Opening the meeting and initiating check-in

- Helping the group create an agenda of burning issues for the rest of the meeting

- Encouraging a balance of personal and professional issues

- Making sure that each burning issue is addressed

- Suggesting a change in discussion formats to support diverse learning and communication styles

- Making sure that no one person or group monopolizes the meeting time or tone of the meeting

- Helping the group plan regular community-building activities

- Inviting sharing and discussion on how the meetings are working for all the members

- Helping the group identify and address conflicts

- Inviting someone else to act as facilitator when she wants to participate in the discussion or has her own burning issue

- Suggesting a decision-making process if needed

The facilitator helps individuals do their best thinking by taking care of these tasks:

- Framing the discussion to be of interest to the entire group

- Keeping the discussion focused

- Encouraging all to participate and managing who talks when

- Listening carefully, being patient, asking questions, inviting members to fully express their ideas, and using other appropriate facilitative skills

- Summarizing comments to focus discussion and simplify chart writing

Equipment needed:

- Flip chart

- An easel to hold the chart paper (handy but not necessary)

- Markers

tips

COMMON THINGS A FACILITATOR SAYS:

- "Welcome, everyone."

- "Let's break into pairs for a few minutes."

- "These are really good ideas. Should we make a list?"

- "I'd suggest that we use multi-voting to decide."

- "Last thoughts on this topic before we move on?"

- "Let's have a go-around to see where everyone stands on this."

- "I think Karen was next."

- "Tell us more."

- "It sounds like . . ."

- "Thank you for sharing that."

- "What do you need from the group?"

- "There are a few people who haven't had a chance to speak. Do any of you have a comment?"

- "Does anyone have a different point of view?"

- "Many thanks for hosting the meeting!"

Facilitator's Guide to Participatory Decision Making by Sam Kaner, Lenny Lind, Catherine Toldi, Sarah Fisk, and Duane Berger is an excellent resource for decision making and facilitation.

When I first started in the role of facilitator, I was very nervous. And I started to take everything on my shoulders, because one of my worst fears is asking people for help. I think it was around my third meeting as facilitator that I realized that everybody was in charge of making the meeting a success. Whether I was off or on that night didn't matter completely because there were others there who would volunteer to take on supportive roles and away we'd go! It wasn't me. I couldn't take full credit for it, but it also takes a lot off your shoulders.

Timekeeper

The timekeeper helps the group manage time during the meeting and respect the time agreements they have made. This role is very challenging for some and easy for others. It can be a significant way for some members to step into a leadership role with the group. A member may want to keep the role and practice timekeeping for a while. Another option is to ask for a different volunteer timekeeper at every meeting.

The timekeeper shares leadership responsibilities by taking care of these tasks:

- Helping the facilitator start the meeting on time

- Timing check-in so everyone gets the same amount of time and no one speaks indefinitely

- Calling the group back from eating and socializing at the time agreed upon by the group

- Giving regular updates to keep the group informed of how much time is left for a particular discussion or activity

- Foreshadowing the end of the meeting with a ten-minute warning

- Helping the facilitator end the meeting on time

Equipment needed:

- A timer that is easy to read and operate. It needs to be able to time minutes and seconds. Choose one with a ring that is audible but gentle.

tips

COMMON THINGS A TIMEKEEPER SAYS:

- "Time to get started, everyone!"

- "How much time for check-in today? How many members are here?"

- "How much time should we spend on this topic?"

- "We have about five minutes left."

- "Time is up."

- "Do we need more time?"

- "The meeting ends in ten minutes. Let's wrap up so that those who need to leave can do so."

I love having the electronic timer because it decides who or what to interrupt—I don't have to. I don't like to interrupt people because I think everything someone has to say is important. Being the timekeeper is probably my favorite job. I think I like the detailed nature of managing the time for the group.

Meeting Host

The meeting host arranges for a comfortable meeting environment and for refreshments at the meeting. Some groups meet in providers' homes and agree that the meeting host role will change monthly depending on where the meeting takes place. Some groups decide to have the person hosting the meeting at her house arrange for drinks and a different person bring the food to the meeting. If groups meet in a public building, the meeting host's job includes arriving in time to open the room, providing any signage, arranging the chairs in a circle, and setting up refreshments. If your group provides child care, the meeting host may work with a partner who arranges the child care space and for caregivers for the children.

The meeting host shares leadership by taking care of these tasks:

- Making sure directions to the meeting location and any special parking arrangements are given to the note taker to include in the minutes

- Arranging for food and drinks to be served at the meeting, taking care to accommodate members with special diets or allergies

- Arranging a space for child care and confirming caregivers for the children if the group provides child care

- Setting up the environment—chairs in a circle, flip chart and announcements board setup, etc.

- Arranging for comfortable temperature and control of excess noise

- Greeting people upon arrival

- Pointing out the bathroom and where to put coats

- Welcoming and introducing new people

- Providing name tags when new people attend or when the group has a speaker

- Inviting members to see her child care space if the meeting is held in her home

- Announcing personal boundaries concerning family space, time, privacy, and noise if the meeting is held in her home

- Arranging for cleanup

COMMON THINGS A MEETING HOST SAYS:

· "Welcome!"

· "Feel free to look at my day care space."

· "My family is at my daughter's basketball game. They will be home later."

· "The decaf is labeled."

· "We'll need to be done right at 9:00 tonight."

· "Would a few people please volunteer to help with cleanup?"

I feel really proud when my support group meeting is at my house. The other providers get a chance to see my space and I enjoy their compliments! It is a lot of work to have the house tidy and to make a snack, but it's worth it when my friends and I are together.

The Role of Individual Group Member

Each member of the group shares leadership by paying attention, staying engaged, being willing to speak about what's true for her, and stepping up to support the group or individuals when she sees a need. Each member takes the lead in balancing her own needs with the needs of other providers and with the needs of the group as a whole. Christina Baldwin, author of *Calling the Circle,* describes this process as taking one's own needs out of the center of the circle and blending them into the edge, creating community with other members, and trusting that together you will hold the circle for the group to do its important work.

All members play an important leadership role in the group by taking care of these tasks:

- Taking responsibility to be present at meetings

- Informing the meeting host ahead of time about lateness or absence

- Reaching out and engaging with new members in a genuine way

- Reaching out to all other members to build friendship and community

- Participating in forming group values and standards and following them

- Respecting the efforts of those who have volunteered for specific roles in managing the group's process

- Supporting the facilitator, timekeeper, meeting host, and others by reminding/suggesting/asking/volunteering/informing when there is a need

- Listening to others with full attention

- Drawing out and making space for others' ideas and contributions

- Contributing to discussions with brief and honest comments

- Sharing the reasons behind personal opinions

- Letting go of needing to be right and respecting the many differences between people

- Appreciating other members

- Contacting other members in between meetings for conversation and support

- Maintaining strict confidentiality

COMMON THINGS GROUP MEMBERS SAY:

- "It's good to see you!"

- "C'mon. It's time to get started."

- "I'll call the members who aren't here this month."

- "I've got a burning issue today. I need some time."

- "It feels like we're off on a tangent. Let's refocus."

- "How much time do we have left?"

- "It looks like you have something to say, Abby."

- "Could we break into small groups to cover these topics?"

- "I appreciate your feedback."

- "Thanks for hosting!"

Facilitator, timekeeper, meeting host, and engaged group members are the fundamental roles that all groups sharing leadership will want to learn about. To get started, one person may be filling several of these roles. Before you know it, however, others will come forward to participate, and you will be well on your way to sharing and building leadership with your entire group all the time.

More Reading

Gonzalez-Mena, Janet. 1993. *Multicultural issues in child care.* Mountain View, Calif.: Mayfield Publishing Company.

This excellent book takes an in-depth look at how caregivers and parents can share leadership and make decisions about children's care. The concepts and strategies Ms. Gonzalez-Mena presents are compelling for family child care providers' work with parents and with their support group colleagues.

Matrixx System® COLORS Training.

In this two- to three-hour interactive workshop, participants identify their own communication and personality style and learn about other people's styles as well. It is based on the Myers-Briggs personality profile tool but is a lot more fun(!), and participants end up with a system that they can remember and use in their work with parents and colleagues.

Nine

Learning More Shared Leadership Roles

Note Taker, Chart Writer, Outreach Coordinator, Process Monitor

Rather than directing their "followers" as traditional leaders do, these (community) leaders ask good questions and draw out people's thinking so they can find their own direction. Leaders from the less understood tradition are not so interested in mobilizing followers as they are in supporting oppressed people to develop their own leadership capacities. They are . . . community othermothers who uplift their neighbors by supporting their development as human beings.

Mary Field Belenky, Lynne A. Bond, Jacqueline S. Weinstock
in *The Tradition That Has No Name*

In the last few chapters, we discussed shared leadership in general and the roles of facilitator, timekeeper, meeting host, and each group member in detail. In this chapter, we'll discuss four more roles that your family child care support group may want to add to its shared leadership structure:

- Note Taker
- Chart Writer
- Outreach Coordinator
- Process Monitor

Note Taker

The note taker is responsible for keeping all members informed about current and upcoming meetings. She sends out minutes by mail or e-mail, taking care to accommodate any special needs that members may have, such as impaired vision or being more comfortable with a different language.

The note taker needs to be very careful to respect the confidentiality of the members at the meeting. No part of check-in should be recorded or shared outside the meeting without permission from the speaker. Names should not be mentioned in association with the burning issues discussed at the meeting without permission from the participants.

In our support group, determining the best time to send out the minutes required trial and error. We found that receiving minutes one to two weeks before the next meeting worked well. It served as a good reminder for the upcoming meeting and as a refresher of the last meeting. There is also something to be said for receiving minutes immediately after the meeting. It includes those who were absent and keeps them up-to-date. With e-mail, it is easy to send another reminder closer to the next meeting. Your group should experiment and evaluate as you go along.

The distribution of minutes is one important way the group stays in touch. Since it takes some organization to get the e-mail distribution lists and/or mailing lists set up, the note taker usually keeps this role for a year or so. The minutes are more likely to be delivered to everyone on time when you have one person doing it consistently for a while rather than passing the responsibility to different people from month to month.

In the note taker role, we see once again how the skills a provider learns as she fills different roles in a shared leadership model can be transferred into other leadership positions. The note taker role requires skills and sensitivities that are particularly important when working with parents and other groups—i.e., being sensitive to the best way for individuals to receive information, ensuring confidentiality, and paying attention to timeliness of the communication. These are all critical considerations in building trust with parents, other adults, and fellow support group members.

The note taker prepares minutes and shares leadership by taking care of these tasks:

- Recording the date and place of the meeting

- Recording the names of the members in attendance

- Expressing appreciation to the meeting host

- Listing the topics and main points of each discussion

- Recording any decisions that are made

- Listing any actions to be taken or tasks to be performed and who is responsible for them

- Listing any issues to be carried over to future meetings

- Recording announcements from the meeting

- Noting the date and place of the next meeting

- Sending out the minutes to all members so that they receive them one to two weeks before the next meeting

Equipment needed:

- Paper, pen

- List of members' home and e-mail addresses

- Internet access

- Envelopes, stamps

When I started in Sojourn, I think the roles were pretty well explained and established so I felt all right stepping into any role, except facilitator. I feel I am only asked to do what I am comfortable with, and not everyone has to have a role. I took on the role of note taker early on and felt I was of real service to the group.

COMMON THINGS THE NOTE TAKER SAYS DURING THE MEETING:

- "Please sign in on this sheet."

- "Please check this list to see if I have your correct address and/or e-mail address."

- "Please let me know how you would prefer to receive the minutes."

- "If you have announcements, please give me a copy for the minutes."

- "Could you please repeat that? I didn't catch all of it."

- "I'd like to double-check the date and place of the next meeting."

Chart Writer

The chart writer takes responsibility for creating large visual records of the groups' work so the whole group can stay organized and focused. Generally, the chart writer records three things:

- Agenda items, including individuals' burning issues as they are added at the meeting

- Notes from some group discussions

- Brainstorming lists, charts, etc., for decision-making purposes

As members mention the issues they would like to discuss that evening, the chart writer notes them in the appropriate part of the flip chart agenda. Seeing the issues written down usually makes members feel reassured that their concerns will not be forgotten.

Capturing the points made during a discussion validates everyone's contribution equally. Writing down the ideas provides the members with a record of what has been said so no one has to worry about remembering everything; they can just glance at the flip chart to get the whole picture again. Often the note taker uses the list to summarize the discussion for the minutes. The person who requested the discussion will appreciate taking home the list of main points to look over later.

The chart writer plays a particularly important role when the group makes decisions. Creating visual lists, groupings, priorities, and choices is critical to participatory decision making.

The chart writer is a role that can easily be passed around from month to month, but be sure to allow members the opportunity to practice for several months if they would like to develop their chart-writing abilities. These are very valuable skills that have application in many community groups and educational settings.

GUIDELINES FOR CREATING UNDERSTANDABLE CHARTS:

(adapted from *Facilitator's Guide to Participatory Decision Making* (1996) by Sam Kaner, Lenny Lind, Catherine Toldi, Sarah Fisk, and Duane Berger)

- Print your letters in plain block capitals.

- Use a thick-lined marker.

- Write straight up and down.

- Change colors between ideas or topics.

- Use green, blue, purple, or brown for text.

- Save pink, red, and orange for highlighting text or for titles.

- Avoid using black.

- Use nouns and verbs. Charts should be understandable to someone who wasn't at the meeting. Example: Instead of writing "schedule/environment" write "Consider changing schedule and/or environment."

- Use stars, circles, boxes, and underlining to emphasize important ideas.

The chart writer shares leadership by taking care of these tasks:

- Helping the group create an agenda that includes the members' current burning issues and business items

- Capturing comments during an open discussion

- Noting ideas that the group wants to discuss at a later time. This list is often called the "parking lot."

- Validating, equalizing, and balancing everyone's contributions

- Creating a group memory

- Creating a visual aid that may help some members participate more fully

- Allowing the note taker to participate in the discussion

- Giving a member a written reminder of the discussion about her burning issue

- Helping the group make decisions by capturing brainstorming, prioritizing, etc.

- Rolling up and labeling decision-making charts in order to be able to continue at the next meeting

Equipment needed:

- Large flip chart paper

- An easel to hold the paper (very handy but not absolutely necessary)

- Bold colored markers (chart-writing markers with chiseled tips work best, but any markers that make thick lines will do)

tips
_____

COMMON THINGS CHART WRITERS SAY:

- "I missed that last comment. Could you please repeat it?"

- "Did I capture what you meant here?"

- "Would you like this list to take home?"

- "I'll bring these charts to the next meeting.

I am kind of an organization nut, so the chart writer role fits me well. I also feel good knowing that I am good at it and that it really helps the group stay on topic during a discussion. It's a great feeling to hand someone a chart full of ideas for her to take home when the meeting is over.

Outreach Coordinator

Mutual support and community building goes on both during and between support group meetings. The outreach coordinator supports communication and community building between meetings in a variety of ways. The outreach coordinator uses the telephone, e-mail, and cards to reach out to members who were absent from each meeting. She helps members pass on information quickly by organizing a telephone tree or e-mail distribution list. She may also acknowledge special events and coordinate support for members going through difficult times.

Each family child care support group will settle on a different way to share this role. Some groups have one person manage the telephone tree and another acknowledge special events. Many groups ask different members to volunteer each month to call the colleagues who missed the meeting.

The outreach coordinator shares leadership by taking on these tasks:

- Calling members who have missed a meeting to check in with them and share what happened at the meeting

- Coordinating the giving of cards and gifts for special occasions

- Coordinating help for members who are experiencing sickness or other difficulties

- Creating a telephone tree and/or e-mail distribution list for passing on information quickly to all members, and distributing a copy of those lists to all members

- Making sure that new members receive information about group guidelines, rituals, and expectations, and about shared leadership

SAMPLE TELEPHONE TREE

Adriane 555-1111

Sara 555-2222	Sonia 555-4444	Graciela 555-5555
Mary D. 555-6666	Janelle 555-2333	Tanya 555-8888
LaShondra 555-1222	Carrie 555-7777	Tim 555-3444
*Jane 555-9999	*Kim 555-0000	*Anne 555-1234

Directions for the telephone tree:

Adriane starts the telephone tree by making three calls: one to Sara, one to Sonia, and one to Graciela.

Then Sara, Sonia, and Graciela each make one phone call to the next person on the list. If she reaches that person (for Sara this would be Mary D.), she is done. That person calls the next person, and so on til the end of the list. If anyone doesn't answer, the caller leaves a message and calls the next person on the list until she reaches a live person. The last member in each column (names with an *) calls the person at the top of the list, in this case Adriane, to confirm that the message made it through.

Last night at a meeting, no one wanted to be the outreach coordinator because there were too many people absent. No one had time to make all of those calls! The facilitator suggested that maybe it was all right to just send out the minutes that month, but I wasn't sure. . . . In the end, we decided to share the responsibility and each call one or two people.

Process Monitor

The role we refer to as process monitor has been called a variety of names by authors describing shared leadership in different settings. John Gastil first described it as "vibes watcher" in his book *Democracy in Small Groups* (1993). Katrina Shields uses that term, too, in *In the Tiger's Mouth: An Empowerment Guide for Social Action* (1994). The National Congress of Neighborhood Women calls it "assistant to the facilitator" in *The Neighborhood Women's Training Sourcebook* (1993). Most recently, Christina Baldwin called this role "guardian of the circle" in her book *Calling the Circle* (1995).

In our version, the process monitor respectfully backs up the facilitator and timekeeper by specifically watching the process and flow of the meeting. She keeps in mind the guidelines for interaction that the group agreed to follow. She calls the group's attention to gaps between their expectations for the group and the process currently unfolding. She can also suggest, in a positive way, possible next steps to move along the group's process.

The process monitor looks to achieve a balance between the work of the group as a whole and the needs of individuals. She takes special care to be respectful of the timekeeper and facilitator as she communicates in a reflective and nonjudgmental way what she is noticing in the group's process as a whole.

Again, this is not unlike the work of a family child care provider who needs to look out for the good of the whole group of children while also supporting positive growth and development for each child.

Some people find this role very difficult, while others find it a natural fit. At first, it would probably be best for a member to practice watching and reflecting on the group's process for several months in a row. Later, when most members have a good idea of how it feels to engage everyone in discussion, be respectful with time and words, and share leadership, different volunteers can fill the role from month to month. Assigning this role to one individual does not take away the responsibility of every member to be watching the process and speaking up for group and individual needs.

The process monitor shares the leadership of the group by taking on the following tasks:

- Focusing on process

The facilitator focuses on helping each member do her best thinking, feeling, speaking, and listening. The timekeeper helps the group keep its agreements about the use of time. The process monitor supports the facilitator, timekeeper, and the group by watching that the process is working for most of the group and is appropriate for the current topic.

- Noticing if the group members are abiding by the agreements they've made about interacting with one another

- Noticing that an agreed-upon rule or structure is not being followed and asking the group members if they mean to be changing it

- Being sensitive to opportunities for community building

- Attending to the "vibes" of the group. Are members tired? Hungry? Restless? Is someone angry? Disengaged?

- Conferring with the facilitator about a change in activity, format, setting, or agenda to improve the group's interaction and participatory process

tips
_____

COMMON THINGS THE PROCESS MONITOR SAYS:

- "This is such an exciting topic that we've been interrupting one another at times. Let's remember to take turns talking."

- "I'm hearing three points of view on this topic. Maybe we could group the comments under those three headings."

- "It feels like we're rushed. Are we attempting to cover too much in one meeting?"

- "I've noticed that we're taking a long time getting settled after break. Should we lengthen the time we schedule for eating and socializing?"

- "How about a one-word go-around to collect the feelings in the room right now?"

Let's take this idea of being a process monitor into the parent-provider relationship for a moment. The part of that role that transfers most powerfully is that the provider becomes responsible to invite conversations with parents—whether easy or difficult ones. For example, just as the process monitor notices the big picture in the support group meeting and brings it to the attention of the group, a provider might notice a pattern and say to a parent, "I've noticed that your family hasn't been able to make any of our group get-togethers. I would love for you to be able to come. Tell me how this is working for your family. I would like to see if I can help make it easier for you." We can't force anyone—colleague or parent—into trusting relationships, but we can do our part by leading, inviting, and modeling in a sensitive way how open, reciprocal relationships get established and maintained.

The roles of note taker, chart writer, outreach coordinator, and process monitor help support the work of the family child care support group while building leadership skills in its members that apply to both individuals and groups. It is very important to remember that even though individual members volunteer to take these responsibilities, all members remain responsible for watching the process and speaking up for group and individual needs all the time. Shared leadership means that everyone is a leader.

When I'm the process monitor, it's all about the group—it's not about the individual. I think many providers have a good awareness of the "big picture" for the flow of things and how to accommodate everyone. The role of process monitor is very freeing for me because I am so good at these skills. I don't like paying attention to the minute detail of the timekeeping, but I can pay attention to the big picture of the process and flow of the meeting. Clearly, there are different personalities for different roles!

More Reading

Belenky, Mary Field, Lynne A. Bond, and Jacqueline S. Weinstock. 1997. *The tradition that has no name.* New York: HarperCollins.

This book is a fascinating study of a tradition in African American communities for some older women to encourage the development of leadership capacity in others. Their particular brand of leadership development ends up benefiting not only the individuals but also the entire community.

Wheatley, Margaret J. 1992. *Leadership and the new science: Learning about organizations from an orderly universe.* San Francisco: Berrett-Kohler.

As we read this compelling book comparing organizations to subatomic particles, we kept seeing our own little family child care groups described. In Ms. Wheatley's book, we are the "strange attractors" because we keep the little excitable particles from zooming off helter-skelter. It made us think that if someone wanted to hire managers who understood how to share power and allow individuals freedom to develop without creating chaos, they should interview family child care providers!

Ten

Making Discussions Worthwhile

In almost all groups, two or three people talk most of the time,

most of the people comment occasionally, and a few individuals

never talk at all.

Cathy Toldi, author, facilitation trainer, and senior associate with Community at Work

Open discussion is the way most groups talk about most topics. It is the unstructured, conversational way in which people usually interact. In open discussion, one person brings up a subject and talks for as long as she'd like. The speakers who follow talk about the same topic or may change the subject slightly. The conversation may deepen or may go off in different directions depending on the interests of each participant. Members of your family child care support group will naturally discuss issues in this unstructured, conversational way. Open discussion will work well for some of your members and not so well for others.

Some people are very comfortable with the free-for-all nature of open discussion. They have no trouble speaking up in groups and voicing their feelings and opinions. As in all groups, there will be a handful of people in your family child care support group who do most of the talking during open discussion. Most of your members will make a few comments, and some will just listen.

For many people, open discussion is intimidating. Some people are afraid they will have to defend themselves if they speak up. Some need a chance to pull their own thoughts together before speaking in a group. Some are hesitant to express a viewpoint that is contrary to what others are saying. For many reasons, open discussion does not really feel open to everyone. To support learning, encourage personal development, and include diverse points of view in family child care support groups, we need to find a way for all members to participate comfortably in open discussion.

In this chapter, we will first look at how to make open discussion more inclusive. Later in the chapter, we will talk about things to try if your group is running into difficult dynamics during open discussion.

When I am with my support group and I have an issue that I really want advice about, I know I can speak up and ask. During an open discussion, it feels so good to say it like it is and not worry that my problem will be judged or shot down. I feel so safe—it's a great feeling. Open discussion helps me to be able to verbally process what I'm thinking about an issue and then to hear from others what they think about it. We understand each other and can relate to each other like nobody else can.

Family Child Care Providers Practice Facilitation Skills Every Day

Even though there are many problems with open discussion, it is an important way that groups communicate. Your group will need to learn how to manage the challenges of open discussion. Fortunately, skilled family child care providers are practicing facilitation skills every day as they work with children.

Think of how you interact with the children in your group when they are talking around the lunch table. You encourage them to speak up and share what is on their mind, to listen carefully, and to respond to each other. You summarize what children say and ask questions to draw out more details of their thinking. You make sure that everyone gets a chance to talk. During open discussion in family child care support group meetings, we have the opportunity of being intentional and respectful in a similar way, but this time with our adult colleagues. Naturally, these concepts can be applied to our relationships with parents and other adults as well.

In chapter 4, we discussed how to create an agenda for the support group meeting from the members' current burning issues. After your group has listed the discussion topics for that meeting, decided on their order, and assigned an appropriate amount of time to each, you are ready to open discussion on the first topic. Here are some guidelines to include more of your support group members in open discussion.

Step by Step—Making Open Discussion Worthwhile for Everyone

The facilitator frames the discussion by doing these things:

- Reminding the group of the amount of time you have agreed on for discussing that particular topic

- Suggesting that people keep their comments brief so that everyone gets a chance to participate

- Asking someone to record the comments on a flip chart if appropriate

- Inviting the provider whose burning issue is going to be discussed to start the discussion by giving a short description of the issue and defining what she'd like from the group

The facilitator or any member can encourage participation and deeper thinking as the conversation goes along. For example, anyone can make comments like these:

- "Tell us more about that."

- "You're emphasizing that because . . . ?"

- "Does someone have a different way of looking at this issue?"

- "Let's hear from folks who haven't spoken for a while."

- "Jackie, you look like you have something to say."

- "We have five minutes left. Can we hear from those who haven't spoken yet?"

- "I think I hear two main ideas in our discussion. They are . . . Does that sound right to the rest of you?"

The facilitator or another member can check with the provider who requested the discussion to see if the discussion is meeting her needs. The time-keeper gives a two- to three-minute warning. The group can decide to continue the discussion for a specific amount of time if appropriate. To close, suggest a quick go-around—one word or one sentence—to allow each member to give her last few thoughts or feelings on the subject. This is especially helpful if there has been some disagreement or a wide variety of ideas brought forward.

tips

When you engage in open discussion in your family child care support group, the group members may need help remembering two things:

- To encourage everyone to participate in the conversation

- To stay focused on the topic being discussed

Encouraging Full Participation Using a Technique Called Stacking

This technique is adapted from *Facilitator's Guide to Participatory Decision Making* by Kaner, Lind, Toldi, Fisk, and Berger (1996).

Stacking is another name for taking turns. When the conversation is animated, you can encourage better listening and fuller participation by gently naming the order of the next few speakers. This list of two to four names is called the "stack." When people hear their name in the stack and are sure that they will get a chance to talk, they can relax and listen to what others are saying while they wait for their turn. Those who are not in the queue—or stack—can relax, too, because they know how to get into the conversation without having to interrupt someone. You can very gently begin stacking a conversation when you see that only a few people are talking but that others want to participate. Listen in on a conversation in which the stacking technique is used:

Facilitator: "Who would like to speak next?" Several members raise their hands. The facilitator points to those with raised hands, saying, "First Sarah, then Della, and then Kim."

Sarah, Della, and Kim take turns talking. The facilitator says, "Who has some other ideas on this topic?" Several members raise their hands. The facilitator says, "Francie, Adriane, then Alexa."

Marisol says, "Could I say this quickly before we go on? It pertains to the last comment."

Francie responds, "Okay. Really quick!"

Marisol makes her comment. The facilitator says, "Thanks, Marisol. Francie . . ."

Stay Focused by Framing the Topic for Interesting Discussion

When everyone is interested in the discussion topic, the group is more likely to stay focused and not get into side conversations or move off into other issues. When a topic is so broad and undefined that some members are not engaged, you may need to narrow the topic down into something the group can work on together.

For example, in September, group members may be stressed with all the demands of starting new families and transitioning children. Instead of talking about this stress in vague generalities or as a list of complaints, you could suggest teasing out the ways providers manage these transitions. Example: "We have a lot of providers who have started new children this month. How about if we focus our discussion on specific strategies we've used for helping children, parents, and ourselves feel comfortable during the first few weeks of care?"

On the other hand, sometimes the topic is too specific to be useful to everyone. For example, when a provider is having ongoing problems with a parent paying late, instead of discussing that particular parent, you may want to expand the conversation to encourage providers to share their experiences with the parent-provider relationship in a more general way. For example, you might say, "Paying late is a real problem. Let's discuss ways we communicate clearly with parents to avoid that problem and also options we have when the conflict does come up. Who would like to share an example of one of those situations?"

---

tips

FRAMING OPEN DISCUSSIONS

Use the following guidelines to frame open discussions:

If the topic is vague	Discuss a *specific* aspect
If the topic is too specific	Discuss a *larger issue* that relates to it
If there is controversy	Chart the different views
If there are complaints	Chart them and add possibilities for taking action
If someone needs advice	Ask open-ended questions and tell stories from experience

Tackling Common Problems during Open Discussion

Some of these suggestions are adapted from *Facilitator's Guide to Participatory Decision Making* by Kaner, Lind, Toldi, Fisk, and Berger (1996).

PROBLEM: The meeting runs overtime.

Try:

- Agreeing on times for each item on the agenda and asking a time-keeper to help the group respect that decision

- Starting the meeting earlier

- Planning a shorter agenda

PROBLEM: A few people are dominating the discussion.

Try:

- Stacking the discussion

- Asking to hear from members who haven't spoken or who might have an idea that hasn't come up yet

- Suggesting an alternative to open discussion. Example: Talk in pairs; go around the group; role-play. Check out more ideas in part two of chapter 11.

PROBLEM: Members change the subject.

Try:

- Reminding the group of the topic at hand and suggesting that the new topic be added to the "burning issues" list for next time

- Reframing the discussion to clarify the subject at hand

PROBLEM: Providers are telling each other what to do.

Try:

- Modeling using facilitative skills (see chapter 7)

- Suggesting that members ask open-ended questions, stick to "I" statements, and share personal experience (see chapter 7)

- Brainstorming how you help children think through issues and applying those concepts to adults

PROBLEM: People are interrupting each other or having side conversations.

Try:

- Stacking the discussion
- Changing to another discussion format (see chapter 11)
- Planning for more socializing time

PROBLEM: The group is large.

Try:

- Breaking into smaller groups
- Stacking the discussion
- Using a fishbowl for discussion (see chapter 11)

More Reading

Vella, Jane. 1994. *Learning to listen, learning to teach: The power of dialogue in educating adults.* San Francisco: Jossey-Bass.

The first two chapters of this book give a solid overview of the things you'll want to keep in mind as you go about learning concepts and skills of shared leadership, as well as anything else with your group. Some of the topics covered are needs defined by the participants, safety, sound relationships, action and reflection, respect for learners, feelings, clear roles, teamwork, and engagement. This book gives you a glimpse into the potential that meaningful conversation in your family child care support groups has for your members' growth and education—and for building reciprocal relationships with parents.

Eleven

Opening Up
the Discussion

If your group mostly talks, doing something physical or spiritual,

or introducing music or art can bring new life.

Tova Green in *Insight and Action*

Even though open discussion is the most common way that adults interact in a group setting, there are many other ways we can structure interactions. In this book, we call these other structures "alternatives to open discussion" and we call moving from one to another "changing formats." In this section, we'll discuss the importance of using these alternatives, which ones to choose for different situations, and suggestions for changing from one format to another.

To understand why using a variety of discussion formats is so important for groups, think about your work with young children. It is clear that children have individual ways of learning and being in the world. Some children learn best when they can talk with you about their experiences. Others may speak less but stay very busy exploring with their senses, hands, and bodies. As you plan learning experiences for any group of children, you plan carefully so that all the children in the group have the opportunity to learn and grow in ways that are both comfortable and challenging to each of them individually. Learning experiences for adults should be planned with the same sensitivity.

You will want to keep in mind that adults, just like children, like to learn and express themselves as whole people. They may have a learning style that suits them well in some circumstances and other styles that work better at other times. Including verbal interaction, visual/sensory experiences, and physical activity will allow most members to engage at least some of the time in a lively and confident way.

Let's review the three goals of a family child care support group:

- Encouraging positive, supportive relationships among the members of the group

- Addressing providers' current concerns at the meetings in order to raise the quality of care for children and improve relationships with the children's families

- Building leadership capacity in all the members at every meeting

The goals of the family child care support group will not be met if a group relies on open discussion for most interactions. Some members will disengage and others will dominate. Some members will get meaningful help to improve their care and others will not. Using a variety of alternative discussion formats at every meeting will make your family child care support group a place where all members enjoy themselves, share equally their important views and experiences, learn effectively with each other, and become confident leaders.

As you consider appropriate formats for different situations, be sure to consider the relative safety levels of different activities as well. In general, talking in pairs or groups of three may feel safer for many providers than speaking up in a large group. At first, addressing a specific topic at check-in (focused check-in) will feel safer than deciding on one's own what to share (unfocused check-in). Start with activities that are safest for the group and consult with the group about moving on to formats that may be more challenging.

Basic Alternatives to Open Discussion

Many of these techniques are adapted from *Facilitator's Guide to Participatory Decision Making* by Kaner, Lind, Toldi, Fisk, and Berger (1996).

Here's a list of the alternatives to open discussion that we'll discuss in this chapter:

- Socializing

- Games

- Go-around

- Idea listing or brainstorming

- Talking in pairs

- Individual writing

- Construction or drawing

- Small groups

- A moment of silence to think

- Role-playing

- Fishbowls

Socializing

When to choose:

- Before a meeting

- While eating

Reasons to choose:

- To build community

- To acknowledge providers' desire to visit informally with colleagues

- To allow providers time to admire and get ideas from the meeting host's child care space

- To ensure that the meeting can start on time and stay focused

- To allow providers a chance to discuss issues important to them without taking up the time of the entire group

What to do:

- Plan a half hour of informal socializing time before the scheduled meeting time. Be sure to start the meeting on time.

- Plan for fifteen to twenty minutes for socializing while eating.

Games

When to choose:

- Near the beginning of the meeting

- When the group needs a break in the middle of the meeting

Reasons to choose:

- To build community

- To put members at ease

- To laugh and have fun together

- To connect with old and new friends

- To engage members who like to be physically active

What to do:

- Say, "I have a game that I think you will enjoy. It's called . . ."

- Turn to chapter 3 of this book to find a game to try.

- Be sure to ask group members for suggestions.

Go-Around

When to choose:

- At the beginning or end of a discussion
- At the end of the meeting
- When you want to hear where individual members stand regarding a decision to be made

Reasons to choose:

- To gather lots of ideas quickly
- To discourage monopolizing and include everyone
- To summarize and evaluate
- To allow everyone a "last word" on a hot topic
- To reach closure

What to do:

- Say, "We're almost out of time for this topic. Let's have a go-around. Each person quickly give one sentence that sums up any last thoughts on this topic."
- Say, "Our colleague needs some ideas for summer field trips. Let's start with a go-around. In thirty seconds or less, name your favorite field trip and why you like it."

Idea Listing or Brainstorming

When to choose:

- At the beginning of a discussion
- During decision making

Reasons to choose:

- To jump-start a discussion and get everyone involved
- To generate innovative solutions
- To provide structure for a complicated topic

What to do:

- Set up a flip chart in a central spot. Ask for a volunteer to be the chart writer and give that person a marker.

- Clearly state what kind of list the group will be generating. Example: "Let's create a list of easy-to-make, process-oriented gifts for parents," or "Let's brainstorm ways we can get food to our meetings," or "Let's list the pros and cons of this proposed licensing change."

- Every idea should be written down on the flip chart. The list can be shared in the minutes and used at a later meeting if needed.

Talking in Pairs

When to choose:

- At the beginning of a meeting

- At the beginning or middle of a discussion

Reasons to choose:

- To put a new member at ease

- To make room for quiet members to share comfortably

- To allow talkative members to speak for a longer chunk of time

What to do:

- Ask each person to find a partner.

- State the topic and suggest that each person talk uninterrupted for ninety seconds on that topic. At the end of ninety seconds, announce that the second person should begin. Call time at the end of the second ninety minutes, or

- State the discussion topic and give each pair fifteen minutes to share. Remind them to share the time equally and to use facilitative skills to help each other think more deeply.

- Return to the large group to continue the meeting or for sharing.

Individual Writing

When to choose:

- At the beginning or middle of a discussion

- For evaluation purposes

- For voting

Reasons to choose:

- To give members a chance to collect their thoughts in preparation for listening carefully to others and sharing their ideas

- To preserve anonymity in evaluation and voting

What to do:

- Pass out paper and pens to all members and state clearly what they should think about and write. Example: "Before we get started with our discussion, write down three things that come to mind right off the bat. I want each of us to capture our own thoughts now so that we won't forget them as we listen to others."

- Or, "Let's take a minute to jot down any questions or concerns we still have after this discussion."

- Allow enough time for members to think and write.

- Sharing can follow in pairs, in small groups, in a go-around, or by collecting the papers and compiling the results.

Construction/Drawing

When to choose:

- When the group is looking for creative solutions

- For sharing a vision

Reasons to choose:

- To tap into creative thinking

- To think about the big picture

- To start off a discussion with feelings rather than analysis

- To engage hands and mind at the same time

What to do:

- Make sure there is enough paper and drawing or construction materials (pipe cleaners, playdough, and Lego plastic building blocks all work well) at the meeting for individuals or small groups to use. Example: Suggest to the group, "Before we tackle this issue of our own child in the family child care group, let's each draw a picture of our own child in care as an animal. What animal is your child? Draw the animal in action."

- Or, "In small groups, let's construct how we envision our family child care support group making a difference in our community."

- Allow ample time to create.

- Each person or small group can share with the entire group.

- Members can ask questions to draw out more information.

Small Groups

When to choose:

- Before and during a discussion

Reasons to choose:

- To allow more people to share

- To explore different aspects of an issue quickly

- To deepen understanding of a topic by active participation

- To address many burning issues at the same meeting without short-changing any of them

What to do:

- If there are many burning issues, suggest that the group break up into small discussion groups to address each issue more fully. Ask that people with expertise in a particular issue join the group discussing that issue.

- You can also consider breaking into small groups to address different aspects of one issue, for example, "Let's break into three groups to discuss the provider's, parents', and child's interests in this particular situation. After ten minutes, a member of each group will summarize their discussion."

A Moment of Silence to Think

When to choose:

- Before, during, or after a discussion

Reasons to choose:

- To allow members a chance to think individually before listening or talking

- To give members a chance to settle into their feelings during an emotional exchange or before continuing or closing a complex discussion

- To encourage individuals to consider and trust their own feelings

What to do:

- Say, "Let's take a minute to think quietly about this before we go on."

At one point in Sojourn, we were trying to decide for how long the facilitator should serve, and one member was really strong toward one point of view. I started feeling agitated inside, thinking this wasn't how I had expected it to turn out. So I said out loud, "Could we just sit with this for a moment? Could we just have a moment of silence?" And we did that, and as we got done, I just burst into tears. And I said, "It doesn't matter what the particulars are, I can trust that the group will make the best decision together and I don't have to worry about the outcome." I went from being afraid of losing control to recognizing that these were people I could trust.

Role-playing

When to choose:

- Before, during, or after a discussion

Reasons to choose:

- To allow members a chance to explore and practice challenging interactions and situations

- To understand other perspectives

- To envision solutions together

What to do:

- For example, say, "How about if one of us pretends to be the parent in this situation? You could be yourself and practice listening and drawing out the parent. What do you say?"

- Or, "I have to bring up a difficult topic this week—difficult for me anyway. I would like some time later to set up role-playing and practice how I'm going to approach it. I'd like your feedback from the parent's point of view. I'm afraid I'm being judgmental."

- Or, "Let's set up role-playing with someone as a state licensor, someone as the technical college director, and a couple of us as providers. Let's pretend we're deciding how to improve training for family child care providers and see where it goes."

Fishbowls

When to choose:

- During a discussion

Reasons to choose:

- To slow down a complex discussion

- To allow a large group to think deeply together

- To hear the thoughts of those who have a lot of expertise or experience with a given topic in a structured way

- To focus on the interaction of polarized viewpoints

What to do:

- Put two or three chairs in the middle of the circle facing each other. They are in the fishbowl.

- Providers who are going to speak on that topic sit in the middle. Everyone else will watch and listen quietly for the time being.

- Agree on a time limit for the fishbowl discussion. The discussion proceeds between the two or three participants in the fishbowl until time is called.

- The speakers rejoin the group and listen to reactions from the members.

- Another variation allows for wider participation. When a member in the fishbowl feels like she has said all she'd like to say, she gets up and leaves the inner fishbowl. Someone from the outer circle can then join the fishbowl conversation by simply taking her empty chair.

- Be sure to time the discussion and allow for response from the group afterwards.

Our job as teachers and leaders with families and colleagues often boils down to helping people do their best thinking alone and in groups. Using the facilitative skills you learned about in chapter 7, sensitive facilitation of open discussion, and a variety of alternatives to open discussion will all be important skills in that process.

More Reading

Vella, Jane. 1994. *Learning to listen, learning to teach: The power of dialogue in educating adults.* San Francisco: Jossey-Bass.

This book is written about college teaching but has much to say about the strategies that build trust and a supportive learning environment for family child care support groups too. There is a chapter on facilitating open discussions, one on building trust, and one on teaching adults which would be helpful to those who are leading their group through the process of learning about shared leadership.

Twelve

Supporting Individuals to Take Action

In helping to create the village, you can use advocacy, storytelling,
effective communication, team building, and collaboration with
families and communities. Many of these techniques are already
familiar to you from the work you do with children, . . . and families
every day. These activities provide abundant opportunities for
everyone at every level of early childhood care and education to
lead the way toward better programs, more effective organizations,
and a brighter future for the children in our country.

Debra Ren-Etta Sullivan in *Learning to Lead: Effective*
Leadership Skills for Teachers of Young Children

Before you continue reading in this chapter, please take another look at the quote on the preceding page from Dr. Debra Sullivan's book *Learning to Lead: Effective Leadership Skills for Teachers of Young Children*. What she says in that paragraph is very important as we think about supporting individuals taking action. She emphasizes that individuals *at every level* can take action and lead. Some will take leadership with one person—possibly a spouse or a parent; others with a small group of colleagues or with community or church groups. Some will be working to affect public policy within the field, and other providers will take leadership on their own behalf in their families or in their professional life. Each provider will be ready for a different way to grow and develop as a leader. In the future, as these providers gain experience and confidence, they will step into other leadership roles—some personal and some more public.

Dr. Sullivan also reminds us that the same leadership techniques work whether a provider addresses a community-wide issue or engages with one parent thinking about one child. The concepts that we have been talking about in this book apply to shared leadership across the board.

Support Colleagues to Take Action

Providing high-quality family child care is an enormous and constantly challenging profession in itself. Nevertheless, it is remarkable how many individual providers take on new challenges as they grow in their professional development. Some work on becoming nationally accredited or obtaining a CDA. Others serve on a local, state, or national board. Some may be active in advocacy or association efforts. Another member may be taking college classes, mentoring student teachers, or teaching early care and education classes. Many providers are active leaders in community groups and school and religious organizations. As providers step out into new areas of professionalism and leadership, their family child care support group will be a place where they can be nurtured and encouraged, supported and cheered! This is the group that will listen empathetically to disappointments and join enthusiastically in celebrating achievements.

When one individual member or a small group of members is ready to launch into a higher-education program or a more public leadership role, the support group needs to be ready to support them in a meaningful way. A family child care provider who is looking for, or who has already embarked on, a new professional challenge will bring special needs to the group. At first, she may express frustration, boredom, or anger. Later, she may be afraid or unsure of herself. She may feel that something or someone is holding her back. She may feel overwhelmed or lonely. She may encourage the group to join the effort and want her family child care friends to support her that way. The group should strive to offer a safe place for her to express all these very natural feelings and at the same time encourage her to own them and process them thoughtfully and responsibly.

The group can help the provider acknowledge her feelings and her personal goals, identify her fears, and address the steps she'll need to realize her vision. In this way, the group contributes to her personal and professional development, growth of leadership in the field, and raising the quality of care for children that a highly trained, energized, and confident person offers.

Ways to Support Group Members Taking Action

Much of this material is adapted from *The National Congress of Neighborhood Women's Sourcebook.*

Help your colleague get a vision of her goals.

- Tell us about a time when you felt particularly happy and fulfilled in your work. What in that example would you like to have more of?

- What do you hope for yourself in the year ahead? In the next three years?

- If you reached your vision, how would you feel? What would you have more of?

Help her determine what, if anything, is holding her back.

- What is in the way of your acting to achieve your goal? Family, community, society?

- What are you thinking, feeling, or doing that is building toward your vision?

- What are you doing or feeling that is moving you away from your goal?

Challenge the internal feelings that may be getting in the way.

- Ask the provider about (and remind her of) times when she used the skills and strengths that reaching her new goals will require.

Explore options, resources, skills, training, people.

- What resources and skills do you need to reach your goals?

- What training, money, or time will you need?

- What people would you like to build a relationship with to support you?

Ask, "What support do you need from us?"

- Would role-playing help?

- Would you like one of us to accompany you—and literally stand behind you?

- Would you like to check in with someone on a regular basis?

Check in and celebrate with her as things move along.

Keep Clear about the Goals for Your Family Child Care Support Group

In order to be able to support the members of your group in their work with children and families and in their professional development, it's important to identify the goals for your family child care support group and to keep them firmly in mind. Early in this book, we suggested three goals for family child care support groups:

- Build trust and friendship between group members

- Increase the quality of care for children and the quality of support for their families

- Build leadership for the field of family child care and for our communities

Your group may have some other goals as well. Many support groups function as local associations and many offer formal training at their meetings. Whether you have these goals or others, your group should be careful to guard time for the learning, reflection, and support that is so important in maintaining friendships, high-quality care, and good relationships with parents. If group projects and "business" are allowed to take over the meetings, caregivers may lose the precious opportunity to maintain trusted relationships with other providers. It may become more difficult to get and give support for the teaching, caregiving, program administration, relationships with parents, and personal and professional challenges that make their jobs so challenging and fun!

The support group's main function for creating community, providing support, and building leadership should not be given up lightly. Requests for the group to act together outside of the group meeting will naturally arise from time to time. The group should decide carefully about taking on projects together outside of the support group meetings. Without a doubt, deciding on a project and achieving it together can be a wonderful experience for the group. We challenge you to be intentional and inclusive about making those choices.

In chapter 1, we told you the story of how our support group started and how we came to practice shared leadership. Fast-forward to the present. If you came to one of our meetings today, it might not be clear to you which member is the current facilitator. Members switch off facilitating depending on who wants to take an active part in the discussion. For the first discussion topic, one member will facilitate and someone else will be the chart writer. For the next topic, someone else might facilitate. Members can change roles spontaneously because so many people in the group are comfortable facilitating and filling different roles. They understand that shared leadership means that all members of the group are responsible for the success of the meeting all the time. Whether it's to be timekeeper or chair of an ad hoc committee or note taker, people calmly step up and lead.

Early on, we had a vision that in the future sometime, at a community meeting facilitated by one of our members, someone would whisper to a friend, "Who is she?! She is a fantastic facilitator." And the person would answer, "Oh, she's a family child care provider in the neighborhood. Isn't she great?" We imagined that slowly building shared leadership capacity would end up supporting our members to lead lots of big and little efforts in different areas of their lives—and increase visibility, professionalism, and respect for the field of family child care.

Well, it's happening. Here are some examples:

- One provider says that she used to be defensive and quick to give advice when parents brought up an issue. She thinks that participating in check-in at our support group meetings has helped her learn to be comfortable listening and not hurrying to comment or fix other people's issues. Recently, she got a note from a parent thanking her for "letting her talk and think things through, for being there and just listening."

- One provider uses shared leadership to plan group get-togethers with the families. Previously, she'd set the date independently, but now that she understands the power of community building and shared decision making, she puts up a sign and polls the group to find a date that works for everyone. The first time she did this, the group responded by organizing the potluck and offering to carpool to the event. One hundred percent of the families participated.

- One member offered to lead a discussion group at her synagogue. She discarded the prepared questions and facilitated a more open discussion that the participants loved. They immediately asked that she return to lead more groups.

- One member left family child care and became a kindergarten teacher. As she and her new co-teacher were planning at the beginning of the year, our colleague noticed that they were "spinning their wheels." She offered to chart their discussion as we often do in Sojourn. She began noting their ideas on a flip chart, grouping them by topic, and penciling them into the year's calendar. Teachers from other classrooms came by, marveled at how much planning they were getting done, and sat down to watch how they were doing it.

- One member is part of the leadership team that plans and implements classes and retreats for high school students at her church. During retreats, she implements a version of check-in with the young people and uses facilitative skills constantly in their work together. At one session, she suggested that the kids use an object as a "talking stick" during a discussion—if you had the "stick" in your hand, it was your turn to talk. The kids chose a soda pop bottle as their "talking stick" and had a great discussion.

- One member led a workshop on shared leadership techniques for use during staff meetings at a small private school. The next day, some of the teachers implemented multi-voting and gradients of agreement into their classrooms with their students—the kids loved the sticky dots! The next staff meeting was such an improvement that the director sent our colleague flowers and a $100 honorarium.

- One member uses her facilitation skills in her role as president of our family child care system's advisory board. She skillfully guided the group through revising both the agency's mission statement and substitute care policies.

We envision family child care support groups as places for providers to get the friendship, reflection, and support they need to provide high-quality care for children, to provide effective support for families, and also to develop the leadership skills that are perfectly appropriate for them at a particular time. Each provider is at her own stage of developing voice, confidence, and insight. Support group members can learn to be skilled at providing just the right amount of challenge and support for each individual at her particular stage of leadership development.

Our families and relationships, our profession, and our community organizations all need leadership that is inclusive and values sharing power. By practicing shared leadership in your family child care support group, you can be helping leaders grow for today and for the years ahead. Encouraging providers to build trust and confidence, to practice using their voices to say what is true for them, and to take appropriate leadership steps at their own pace are some of the most important roles your family child care support group can play.

More Reading

Shields, Katrina. 1994. *In the tiger's mouth: An empowerment guide for social action.* Philadelphia: New Society Publishers.

Inspiring and easy-to-read handbook for planning meetings, facilitation, decision making, and taking action. Lots of great strategies for doing the work itself. Reading list is a gold mine for groups or individuals participating in social action.

Sullivan, Debra Ren-Etta. 2003. *Learning to lead: Effective leadership skills for teachers of young children.* St. Paul: Redleaf Press.

We love how Dr. Sullivan sees examples of leadership in everyday interactions with children. Chapter 3, Becoming an Effective Leader, and chapter 4, It Takes a Village, will be of particular interest to providers taking a leadership role with colleagues, with families, and in the community.

Glossary

Accreditation

The highest level of regulation for a family child care program usually awarded by the National Association for Family Child Care (NAFCC). Accreditation standards go well beyond the health and safety standards of state licensing or local certification. NAFCC Accreditation standards were revised in 2002. There are also some local family child care systems that create and monitor their own accreditation standards.

Advocacy

Supporting a cause or proposal, especially, in this case, funding, legislation, and policies that support children, families, and caregivers.

Agenda

A list or outline of things to be considered at a meeting that can include approximate time allotted for each item.

Alternatives to open discussion

Ways of structuring interactions between people that are different than the give-and-take of conversation where people talk in any order for as long as they like. Some examples include talking in pairs, go-arounds, and individual writing.

Association

An organization of family child care providers brought together to meet political and organizational goals. Associations can be organized at the local, state, national, and international levels. Example: Wisconsin Family Child Care Association. Sometimes local family child care associations function informally as a family child care support group too.

Backup care

An arrangement made by the parents of a child in one family child care provider's group to bring that child to a second family child care provider's program when their own caregiver is not available for care.

Barter

Exchanging one commodity or service for another. Example: ten hours of child care exchanged for ten hours of painting. No money is exchanged. The value of the barter is still considered taxable income for tax purposes.

Birth order

The order of siblings from oldest to youngest. The oldest child is first in birth order.

Block

A veto in consensus decision making that does not allow that decision to go forward under any circumstances.

Brainstorming

Gathering as many creative ideas as possible without judgment or analysis.

Burning issue

A current interest or concern that a group member brings to the group for immediate consideration.

CDA (Child Development Associate)

A credential awarded by the National Council for Professional Recognition to an individual rather than a program. CDA recipients must meet educational and competency-based requirements in regards to child development and early care and education.

Changing formats

Moving from one kind of discussion format to a different structure. Example: changing from open discussion to a go-around or changing from individual writing to talking in pairs.

Chart writer

Person who writes down on a flip chart the notes from an open discussion or material during a decision-making process.

Check-in

A special kind of go-around for the beginning of a meeting. Each person in the group has a specific amount of time to share and reconnect—usually one to two minutes.

Class

A group sharing the same economic or social status.

Community

A group of people with something in common—such as all being family child care providers—who also feel trust and connection to one another and as a group.

Confidentiality

Keeping strictly private information having to do with individual people. Anything said during check-in should be kept confidential.

Continuing education hours

Hours spent in non-formalized (non-credit-bearing) educational programming. Licensed family child care providers are required to accumulate a certain number of continuing education hours every year.

CPR

Cardiopulmonary resuscitation (CPR) training is often required for regulated family child care providers. It is a method for restarting the heart with manual chest compressions.

Credential

Awarded to a person after meeting substantial formal educational, practical, and classroom (face-to-face or at a distance) requirements in a specific area. Example: Infant/Toddler credential, Administrator's credential.

Debrief

To discuss something after it happens in order to understand the experience better and deepen the meaning.

Directive leadership

A style of leadership characterized by one person or a small group of people managing, coaching, and giving directions. A directive leader may have more knowledge and thus power in the relationship, but it is not absolute power as in the case of an authoritarian leader.

Discussion formats

Ways to conduct discussion. Example: small groups, writing, brainstorming, open discussion.

Equipment exchange

A program for sharing equipment such as cribs, climbers, strollers, blocks, etc., between family child care providers.

Ethnic origin

Relating to large groups of people grouped according to common racial, national, tribal, religious, linguistic, or cultural origin or background.

Facilitative leadership

A style of leadership that focuses on the individual strengths of each person and encourages and develops leadership ability in each. From *Learning to Lead* by Dr. Debra Ren-Etta Sullivan.

Facilitator

A person who plans and manages the process for a group in order for it to have productive meetings, in-depth discussions, and effective decision-making processes. The facilitation role for planning meetings can be filled by one person for one to two years. The part of facilitation that helps with the process for in-depth discussions and decision making needs to be passed around depending on the topic. The facilitator for a specific discussion needs to be objective and nonjudgmental about that topic.

Family child care associations

Organizations that provide an organizational structure for family child care accreditation, research, training, and political advocacy.

Family child care networks

Loosely describes a variety of family child care gatherings. Networks are local and relatively small. They bring together a group of providers for a specific purpose having to do with support and education.

Family child care support groups

A group that brings together a small number of family child care providers for informal socializing, intentional networking, grassroots leadership development, and supportive peer mentoring on a monthly basis. Some family child care support groups also provide continuing education for their members.

Family child care systems

Formal membership organizations. Systems have their own rules and regulations defining quality standards for the children's care, the providers' training, and/or other specific conditions for membership. Example: U.S. Marine Corps Family Child Care System.

Fishbowl

A discussion format that asks a small number of the group members to discuss a particular topic while the rest of the group watches and listens without participating.

Flip chart

A large two-by-three-foot pad of paper that is mounted on an easel so that all members can see it. Alternatives include taping a large piece of paper to the wall or using large sticky pads of flip chart paper that stick onto the wall. You can buy flip chart paper and easels at office supply stores.

Focused check-in

Check-in that has a specific topic that all members respond to when it is their turn to talk. Example: What are the rituals you have in your group to celebrate the children's birthdays?

Gender

The behavioral, cultural, or psychological traits usually associated with one sex. Example: It is women in western culture who wear skirts.

Go-around

A participatory technique used in small groups where each person speaks briefly one after the next. Usually a go-around proceeds in order around the circle, but variations abound.

Gossiping

Revealing personal or sensational facts about others without their permission and without their knowledge. Gossiping does not belong at family child care support groups. Everything said at family child care support group check-in must be kept confidential. Other conversations should not be attributed to a specific individual. Gossiping about fellow members of a family child care support group undermines trust and community building.

Gradients of Agreement Scale

Used in participatory decision making, a scale of five to eight positions ranging from "whole-hearted endorsement" or "full agreement" to "block" or "refuse this solution." A scale of positions makes it easier for participants to be honest and precise about their opinions. It also allows the group to gauge the level of support for a proposal. This scale was developed at Community at Work in San Francisco.

Group guidelines

A set of expectations for how the group wants to interact with each other. Example of one possible guideline: Keep comments brief.

Hierarchical leadership

Leadership style in which one person or a small group of individuals is in charge and makes most of the decisions.

Individual writing

A discussion format that gives members the opportunity to write down their thoughts individually. Discussion usually follows.

Interrupting the stack

Allowing a person to speak out of turn during an open discussion in which the facilitator is assigning turns to the speakers. Interrupting the stack is encouraged to capture all the comments that deal with a certain topic before moving on to the next person in the stack.

"I" statements

Statements regarding personal feelings, beliefs, opinions, values, practice, etc., that start with "I" and clearly acknowledge that these are not general or universal statements. Example: "I felt sad when they left for kindergarten" is an "I" statement. "You feel sad when kids leave you" is not.

Leadership capacity

The ability of a person or a group to understand, explain, and implement many strategies for helping a group reach its goals. In shared leadership, these strategies would include community building, participatory decision making, implementing roles, and timekeeping.

Logistics

Making decisions and handling the details of an event. Example: the logistics of a meeting.

Longevity

The length of time that a person continues doing family child care. Family child care support groups may increase the longevity of providers in the field.

Meeting host

The person who manages the physical space, refreshments, and comfort of the members at a specific support group meeting.

Minutes

A record of what happened at a support group meeting. The note taker prepares the minutes and sends them out to all the members.

Monopolizing

Controlling a lot of the time during a meeting by talking frequently and for a very long time.

Multi-voting

Casting a vote for more than one of the options in a proposal. Voting this way makes it likely that the winning vote will include more members' choices—be they first, second, or third choices—so more of the members will be supportive of the outcome.

Nonhierarchical leadership

A leadership style in which power is shared by many people. Decision making is inclusive of the ideas of all members, and leadership roles—either formal or nonformalized—are many. It is sometimes called shared leadership.

Note taker

The person who takes notes about what happens at the support group meeting. She prepares a document that includes the minutes and announcements and sends it out to all the members either by mail or e-mail. Notes are not taken during check-in and names are not added to descriptions of burning issues. Example: We discussed biting and came up with these ideas.

Open discussion

The most common type of unstructured conversation in which people speak when they want for as long as they choose, moving from topic to topic in a free-flowing manner.

Open-ended questions

Questions that do not have a factual or "yes" or "no" answer. They allow the person answering to reflect and add their personal experience to the answer. Example: "How does the child's age

affect this issue?" is an open-ended question. "How old is the child?" is not.

Othermothers

Women who guide and care for children and young people other than their own.

Outreach coordinator

The person who agrees to call members who were not at the meeting. The outreach coordinator also sets up the telephone or e-mail tree.

Pair

Two people who talk together, usually about a specified topic for a set amount of time.

Parking lot

A flip chart page or a page in a notebook where topics of interest to the group are "parked" so they won't be forgotten. Groups can decide to address these issues at a later meeting or during a retreat.

Pass

During check-in or other activities, a person may prefer not to speak or participate when her turn comes around. She has the right to stand aside and not share out loud. In that case, she indicates her preference by saying, "Pass."

Peer support

Support between people who have the same job or rank that implies a more equal, sensitive, and practical level of support.

Perceptual learning pattern

Description of the way a person perceives and processes information by ordering her use of kinesthetic, visual, and auditory strategies.

Process monitor

A person in shared leadership groups who acts as backup for the facilitator and the timekeeper. She carefully watches the process, shares what she sees, and, when appropriate, suggests process alternatives that the group may want to consider.

Race

Groupings of people by their skin color and other physical characteristics. Biologists have a hard time defining race, and some believe that there are not actually significant biological markers for race. Nonetheless, race can have a powerful effect on experiences, relationships, perceptions, and group dynamics.

Resource and Referral agency (R&R)

Local and regional agencies that may provide child care certification, training, child care referrals for parents, and sponsorship of the United States Department of Agriculture (USDA) Child and Adult Food Program (CAFP).

Role-playing

Activity where a hypothetical situation is described to the group. Group members volunteer to take the roles of the people in the situation, and then they act out how the situation might unfold.

Safety

The absence of fear, undue stress, or insecurity in a person when invited to participate in an activity.

Shared leadership

Nonhierarchical leadership style. Power and leadership roles are shared or may be rotated among the members.

Stacking

A direct form of turn taking. The facilitator assigns a number to those who would like to speak and calls on each one in turn.

Stereotyping

An idea or mental picture of something that is an oversimplified opinion, prejudiced attitude, or uncritical judgment. Example: Family child care providers are sometimes stereotyped as being uneducated.

Sticky dots

Small, round, colorful stickers available at office supply stores. They are used for multi-voting and employing a Gradients of Agreement Scale.

Team building

Activities, usually games and physical challenges, that require group members to work together and think creatively.

Telephone tree

A system for passing a message on to all the members of a group. Each member calls a specific person or a few specific people, who then do the same until all members are notified.

Template

A format that serves as a pattern and can be used over and over. Example: agenda template.

Timekeeper

The person who agrees to help the group decide how to use its time together and then keeps track of the time in order to help the group abide by its decisions. Example: "Our time is up for this discussion. As I see it, we could either continue next time or take ten more minutes now. What do you think?"

Trust

Believing in the character, ability, strength, or truth of someone.

Unfocused check-in

Check-in that welcomes members to speak about anything they would like to share with the group for a specific amount of time. Unfocused check-in works best with groups that are well established and where trust is high.

USDA

The United States Department of Agriculture (USDA) administers the Child and Adult Food Program (CAFP), which reimburses many regulated family child care providers for some of their child care–related food costs.

Veto

To refuse to approve something. Can also be called a "block" when making decisions by consensus.

Voice

The ability to speak confidently about what is true for you.

Bibliography

Family Child Care

Baker, Amy C., and Lynn A. Manfredi/Petitt. 1998. *Circle of love: Relationships between parents, children, and caregivers in family child care.* St. Paul: Redleaf Press.

Bollin, C. C. 1993. An investigation of job stability and job satisfaction among family child care providers. *Early Childhood Research Quarterly,* 8: 207–220.

Campbell, N. D., J. C. Appelbaum, Karin Martinson, and Emily Martin. 2000. *Be all that we can be: Lessons from the military for improving our nation's child care system.* Washington, D.C.: National Women's Law Center.

Carter, M., and D. Curtis. 1994. *Training teachers: A harvest of theory and practice.* St. Paul: Redleaf Press.

Center for Child Care Workforce. 1999. *Creating better family child care jobs: Model work standards.* Washington, D.C.: Center for Child Care Workforce.

Curtis, Deb, and Margie Carter. 2003. *Designs for living and learning: Transforming early childhood environments.* St. Paul: Redleaf Press.

Family Child Care Accreditation Project. 2002. *Quality standards for NAFCC accreditation.* Salt Lake City: National Association for Family Child Care.

Hamilton, M. E., Mary A. Roach, and David A. Riley. 2003. Moving toward family-centered early care and education: The past, the present, and a glimpse of the future. *Early Childhood Education Journal* 30 (4): 225–232.

Hughes, R. 1985. The informal help-giving of home and center childcare providers. *Family Relations,* 343: 359–366.

Kontos, Susan, C. Howes, M. Shinn, and E. Galinsky. 1994. *Quality in family child care and relative care.* New York: Teachers College Press.

Laurion, Joan. 1996. *Village of kindness: Providing high quality family child care.* Madison: University of Wisconsin Board of Regents.

Modigliani, Kathy, and Ellen Moore. 2004. *Many right ways: Designing your home child care environment. Muchas maneras correctas: Creando su ambiente de cuidado de niños en casa.* St. Paul: Redleaf Press.

Uttal, Lynet. 2002. *Making care work: Employed mothers in the new child care market.* New Brunswick, N.J.: Rutgers University Press.

Weaver, Ruth Harding. 2002. Predictors of quality and commitment in family child care: Provider education, personal resources, and support. *Early Education & Development,* 13 (3): 266–280.

Weaver, Ruth Harding. 2002. The roots of quality care: Strengths of master providers. *Young Children*, 57 (1): 16–22.

Windflower Enterprises. 1993. *Second helping: An advanced enrichment course for family child care providers. (Quatro pasos a una profesión).* Colorado Springs: Windflower Enterprises.

Women's Learning/Feminism

Allen, Pamela. 1970. *Free space: A perspective on the small group in women's liberation.* Washington, N.J.: Times Change Press.

Belenky, Mary Field, Lynne A. Bond, and Jacqueline S. Weinstock. 1991. *The tradition that has no name.* New York: HarperCollins Publishers.

Belenky, Mary Field, Blythe McVicker Clinchy, Nancy Rule Goldberger, and Jill Mattuck Tarule. 1986. *Women's ways of knowing: The development of self, voice, and mind.* New York: HarperCollins Publishers.

Crawford, Mary. 1995. *Talking difference: On gender and language.* London: SAGE Publications.

Gilligan, Carol. 1982. *In a different voice: Psychological theory and women's development.* Cambridge: Harvard University Press.

Goldberger, Nancy Rule, Jill Mattuck Tarule, Blythe McVicker Clinchy, and Mary Field Belenky. 1996. *Knowledge, difference, and power: Essays inspired by women's ways of knowing.* New York: HarperCollins Publishers.

Hayes, Elisabeth, and Daniele D. Flannery, with Ann K. Brooks, Elizabeth J. Tisdell, and Jane M. Hugo. 2000. *Women as learners: The significance of gender in adult learning.* San Francisco: Jossey-Bass.

Helgesen, Sally. 1995. *The female advantage: Women's ways of leadership.* New York: Doubleday Currency.

Luttrell, Wendy. 1997. *School-smart and mother-wise.* New York: Routledge.

National Congress of Neighborhood Women. 1993. *The neighborhood women's training sourcebook.* Columbia, Md.: The Neighborhood Women's Resource Center.

Teske, Robin L., and Mary Ann Tétreault. 2000. *Conscious acts and the politics of social change: Feminist approaches to social movements, community, and power.* Volume One. Columbia, S.C.: University of South Carolina Press.

Community/Team Building

Baker, Amy C., and Lynn A. Manfredi/Petitt. 2004. *Relationships, the heart of quality care.* Washingon D. C.: NAEYC.

Baldwin, Christina. 1994. *Calling the circle: The first and future culture.* New York: Bantam Books.

Fluegelman, Andrew, editor. 1976. *The new games book.* Garden City, N.Y.: Dolphin Books.

Markova, Dawna. 1992. *How your child is smart.* Boston: Conari Press.

Matrixx System® Personality Inventory (Colors) NCTI®, Inc. http://www.ncti.org. 800-622-1644.

Peck, M. Scott. 1987. *The different drum: Community making and peace.* New York: Simon & Schuster.

Rice, Wayne, and Mike Yaconelli. 1986. *Play it!* Grand Rapids: Zondervan Publishing.

Rohnke, Karl, and Steve Butler. 1995. *Quicksilver: Adventure games, initiative problems, trust activities, and guide to effective leadership.* Dubuque: Kendall/Hunt Publishing Company.

Shaffer, Carolyn R., and Kristin Anundsen. 1993. *Creating community anywhere.* New York: G. P. Putnam's Sons.

Snow, Harrison. 1997. *Indoor-outdoor team-building games for trainers.* Blacklick, Ohio: McGraw-Hill.

Starhawk. 1982. *Dreaming the dark.* Boston: Beacon Press.

Facilitation

Coover, Virginia, Ellen Deacon, Charles Esser, and Christopher Moore. 1978. *Resource manual for a living revolution.* Philadelphia: New Society Press.

Hammond, Sue Annis. 1998. *The thin book of appreciative inquiry.* Plano, Texas: Thin Book Publishing Co.

Kaner, Sam, Lenny Lind, Catherine Toldi, Sarah Fisk, and Duane Berger. 1996. *Facilitator's guide to participatory decision making.* Philadelphia: New Society Publishers.

Peavey, Fran. 1994. *By life's grace: Musings on the essence of social change.* Philadelphia: New Society Publishers.

Sher, Barbara, and Annie Gottleib. 1991. *Teamworks!* New York: Warner Books.

Multiculturalism

Barrera, Isaura, Robert M. Corso, and Diane Macpherson. 2003. *Skilled dialogues: Strategies for responding to cultural diversity in early childhood.* Baltimore: Brookes Publishing.

Gonzalez-Mena, Janet. 1993, 1997, 2001. *Multicultural issues in child care.* Mountain View, Calif.: Mayfield Publishing Company.

Schnur, E., R. Koffler, H. G. Wimpenny, H. Giller, and E. N. Rafield. 1995. Family child care and new immigrants: Cultural bridge and support. *Child Welfare,* 74 (6): 1,237–1,248.

Sheared, Vanessa, and Peggy A. Sissel. 2001. *Making space: Merging theory and practice in adult education.* Westport, Conn.: Bergin & Garvey.

Adult Education

Boud, David, and Nod Miller. 1996. *Working with experience: Animating learning.* London: Routledge.

Brookfield, Stephen D. 1990. *The skillful teacher.* San Francisco: Jossey-Bass Publishers.

Donohue, C., and R. Neugebauer. 2004. Innovations in eLearning: Promising practices for early childhood professional development. *Young Children* 59 (3): 22–25.

Freire, Paulo. 1970. *Pedagogy of the oppressed.* New York: Continuum Publishers.

Ishiura, Judy, Susan Gomez, and Diane Harkins. 2001. *The effects of training on family child care providers.* Davis, Calif.: The Center for Human Services, University of California Extension.

Vella, Jane. 1994. *Learning to listen, learning to teach: The power of dialogue in educating adults.* San Francisco: Jossey-Bass.

Leadership and Democracy

Chrislip, David D., and Carl E. Larson. 1994. *Collaborative leadership: How citizens and civic leaders can make a difference.* San Francisco: Jossey-Bass.

Covey, Stephen R. 1990. *Principle-centered leadership.* New York: Simon & Schuster.

Gastil, John. 1993. *Democracy in small groups.* Philadelphia: New Society Publishers.

Green, Tova, and Peter Woodrow, with Fran Peavey. 1994. *Insight and action: How to discover and support a life of integrity and commitment to change.* Philadelphia: New Society Publishers.

Kagan, S. L., and B. T. Bowman. 1997. *Leadership in early care and education.* Washington, D.C.: National Association for the Education of Young Children.

Lakey, B., G. Lakey, R. Napier, and J. Robinson. 1995. *Grassroots and nonprofit leadership.* Gabriola, B.C.: New Society Publishers.

Shields, Katrina. 1994. *In the tiger's mouth: An empowerment guide for social action.* Philadelphia: New Society Publishers.

Sullivan, Debra Ren-Etta. 2003. *Learning to lead: Effective leadership skills for teachers of young children.* St. Paul: Redleaf Press.

Wheatley, Margaret J. 1999. *Leadership and the new science.* San Francisco: Berrett-Koehler Publishers.

WomanSpirit, 2003. Empowering Grassroots Leadership. Circles of Hope, Imani Family Center, 6350 Garesche Avenue, St. Louis, MO 63136-3446. 314-381-1915.

Index Terms

A

accreditation, 3, 4, 135

activities, 6–8, 32–33, 56, 62–66.
See also community-building activities

advice, 69, 77–78, 113

agendas, 38, 43–48, 98, 135

Anyone Who! (game), 28

appreciation, expressions of, 30

attendance at meetings, 4, 60–61

B

Back-to-Back (game), 31–32

balance and balancing, 69, 75–76, 103

Baldwin, Christina, 11, 35

Belenky, Mary F., 20, 95, 105

Berger, Duane, 80

Bond, Lynne A., 95, 105

brainstorming, 77, 98, 119–120, 135

burning issues
    agendas and, 38, 44
    chart writers and, 98, 100
    check-in and, 39, 40
    defined, 135
    facilitators and, 86
    guest speakers and, 53, 54
    as main topics for discussion, 14
    in meeting structure, 47, 49
    note takers and, 96
    too many, 48

C

caregivers, 2, 9

chart writers
    burning issues and, 98
    check-in and, 39
    communication guidelines and, 67–68
    defined, 136
    open discussion and, 109
    in shared leadership model, 13

in support of best thinking, 80
    tasks and tips, 99–100

check-in
    agendas and, 42–43, 46
    defined, 136
    description, 4–5
    focused and unfocused, 40, 42, 117, 137, 141
    guest speakers and, 54, 55
    note takers and, 96
    purpose, 38, 47, 49
    rules for, 39

checklist for guest speakers, 55

child care during meetings, 61, 90–91

Child Development Associate (CDA), 135

circle time, 56, 103

Claytionary (game), 32–33

communication
    exercise, 32
    guidelines for, 67–69, 85, 103
    outreach coordinator and, 101
    styles, exploration of, 29–30

communities, 22–23, 84, 101, 136

community-building activities
    agendas and, 44
    check-in and, 5, 40
    games, 26–35
    learning together, 18
    in meeting structure, 35, 49
    socializing and, 25

confidentiality, 39, 40, 69, 136

conflicts, 59, 75–76

construction activity, 121–122

continuing education hours, 12, 52, 136

CPR (cardiopulmonary resuscitation), 136

D

debrief, 31, 136

decision making, 31, 58, 63–66, 68, 99

dialogue, intentional, 29

differences, honoring, 29–30

discussions
    chart writer and, 98
    domination of, 69, 113
    facilitators and, 85–86
    formats for, 116, 136
    guest speakers and, 53–55
    inclusive, 108
    making space in, 76
    parking lot and, 100
    See also open discussions

drawing, 65, 121–122

drawing out, 74

dues, 61–62

E

eating together, 25, 47, 60

education, 12, 16, 17, 44, 52. *See also* guest speakers

empowerment, 16–17, 131–133

encouragement, 74–75

F

facilitation skills, 72, 79–80

facilitation strategies, 73–78

facilitators
    defined, 137
    in leadership team, 13, 17, 62, 85
    in meetings, 39, 47, 109
    tasks and tips, 86–88

family child care, 3–4, 9, 16, 137

family child care support groups.
    See support groups

finances, 61–62

fishbowls, 124–125, 137

Fisk, Sarah, 80

flexibility, 45

flip charts, 99, 137

focus, maintaining, 111–112

focused check-in, 40, 42, 117, 137

follow-up, 54, 66

food, 4, 25, 47, 60

Four Corners (game), 29–30

framing topics, 111–112

Other Resources from Redleaf

Poking, Pinching and Pretending: Documenting Toddlers' Explorations with Clay

by Dee Smith and Jeanne Goldhaber

Poking, Pinching, and Pretending investigates how one group of infants and toddlers learns about clay as an early "language." Inspired by the programs in Reggio Emilia, this guide encourages educators to share the questions and theories that come from observing and documenting children's interactions with clay to heighten their understanding of how toddlers explore, represent, and learn.

Designs for Living and Learning: Transforming Early Childhood Environments

by Deb Curtis and Margie Carter

Drawing inspiration from a variety of approaches, from Waldorf to Montessori to Reggio to Greenman, Prescott, and Olds, *Designs for Living and Learning* outlines hundreds of ways to create healthy and inviting physical, social, and emotional environments for children in child care.

The Art of Awareness: How Observation Can Transform Your Teaching

by Deb Curtis and Margie Carter

Do more than watch children—be with children. Covering different aspects of children's lives and how to observe them, as well as tips for gathering and preparing documentation, *The Art of Awareness* is an inspiring look at how to see the children in your care—and how to see what they see.

Reflecting Children's Lives: A Handbook for Planning Child-Centered Curriculum

by Deb Curtis and Margie Carter

Keep children and childhood at the center of your curriculum and rethink ideas about scheduling, observation, play, materials, space, and emergent themes with these original approaches.

Theories of Childhood: An Introduction to Dewey, Montessori, Erikson, Piaget, and Vygotsky

by Carol Garhart Mooney

Theories of Childhood examines the work of five groundbreaking educational theorists in relation early education. Each theorist's ideas are presented to help teachers and students look to the foundations of child care for solutions and guidance in classrooms today.

Focused Early Learning: A Planning Framework for Teaching Young Children

by Gaye Gronlund

Focused Early Learning provides a simple and innovative framework for organizing teaching plans into a realistic, classroom-based format that focuses on the unique needs of each child.

800-423-8309
www.redleafpress.org